Alberta's Best Hotels and Restaurants

Travel better, enjoy more

Authors Alexis de Gheldere Jennifer McMorran Lorette Pierson *Contributors:* Mark Heard	**Translation** Myles McKelvey Tracy Kendrick Eric Hamovitch Danielle Gauthier Emmy Pahmer	**Computer Graphics** Stéphanie Routhier **Artistic Director** Patrick Farei (Atoll) **Illustrations** Lorette Pierson
Publisher Pascale Couture **Editor** Jacqueline Grekin	**Page Layout** *Typesetting* Dena Duijkers *Visuals* Isabelle Lalonde	Myriam Gagné Jenny Jasper **Photography** *Cover Page* Anne Gardon
Copy Editing Wayne Hiltz *Editing Assistance* Dena Duijkers	**Cartographers** Patrick Thivierge André Duchesne Bradley Fenton Yanik Landreville *Assistance* Émilie Foy	(Reflexion)

OFFICES

CANADA: Ulysses Travel Guides, 4176 Rue St-Denis, Montréal, Québec, H2W 2M5,
☎ (514) 843-9447 or 1-877-542-7247, ≈(514) 843-9448, info@ulysses.ca,
www.ulyssesguides.com

EUROPE: Les Guides de Voyage Ulysse SARL, BP 159, 75523 Paris Cedex 11, France,
☎ 01 43 38 89 50, ≈01 43 38 89 52, voyage@ulysse.ca, www.ulyssesguides.com

U.S.A.: Ulysses Travel Guides, 305 Madison Avenue, Suite 1166, New York, NY 10165,
☎ 1-877-542-7247, info@ulysses.ca, www.ulyssesguides.com

DISTRIBUTORS

CANADA: Ulysses Books & Maps, 4176 Saint-Denis, Montréal, Québec, H2W 2M5,
☎ (514) 843-9882, ext.2232, 800-748-9171, Fax: 514-843-9448, info@ulysses.ca,
www.ulyssesguides.com

GREAT BRITAIN AND IRELAND: World Leisure Marketing, Unit 11, Newmarket Court, Newmartket Drive, Derby DE24 8NW, ☎ 1 332 57 37 37, Fax: 1 332 57 33 99
office@wlmsales.co.uk

SCANDINAVIA: Scanvik, Esplanaden 8B, 1263 Copenhagen K, DK, ☎ (45) 33.12.77.66,
Fax: (45) 33.91.28.82

SPAIN: Altaïr, Balmes 69, E-08007 Barcelona, ☎ 454 29 66, Fax: 451 25 59,
altair@globalcom.es

SWITZERLAND: Havas Services Suisse, ☎(26) 460 80 60, fax: (26) 460 80 68

U.S.A.: The Globe Pequot Press, 246 Goose Lane, Guilford, CT 06437 - 0480,
☎1-800-243-0495, Fax: 800-820-2329, sales@globe-pequot.com

Other countries, contact Ulysses Books & Maps, 4176 Rue Saint-Denis, Montréal, Québec, H2W 2M5, ☎ (514) 843-9882, ext.2232, 800-748-9171, Fax: 514-843-9448, info@ulysses.ca, www.ulyssesguides.com

No part of this publication may be reproduced in any form or by any means, including photocopying, without the written permission of the publisher.

Canadian Cataloguing-in-Publication Data (see page 6)
© November 2000, Ulysses Travel Guides.
All rights reserved Printed in Canada
ISBN 2-89464-304-7

Table of Contents

Alberta's Best Hotels and Restaurants 9

The Rocky Mountains 15

Calgary 53

Southern Alberta 83

Central Alberta 97

Edmonton 107

Northern Alberta 123

Accommodation Index 130

Restaurant Index 135

Place Index 140

List of Maps

Banff	23
Calgary	55
Centre	59
Enlargement	63
Central Alberta	99
Edmonton	109
Centre	113
Icefields Parkway	35
Jasper	37
Kootenay/ Yoho and Kananaskis Country	47
Lake Louise and Surroundings	31
Lethbridge	90
Medicine Hat	94
Northern Alberta	122
Red Deer	105
Rocky Mountains	17
Southern Alberta	82
Table of Distances	14
Waterton Lakes National Park	86
Where is Alberta	7

Map Symbols

Symbol	Meaning	Symbol	Meaning	Symbol	Meaning
?	Tourist information	◎	Provincial Capital	▲	Campground
✈	Airport	⊠	Border crossing	△	Glacier
🚌	Bus station	⛷	Ski station	▲	Mountain
🚆	Train station	⛳	Golf	☀	Lookout

Symbols

🚢	Ulysses's Favourite
☎	Telephone Number
⇄	Fax Number
≡	Air Conditioning
⊗	Fan
≈	Pool
ℜ	Restaurant
ℝ	Refrigerator
K	Kitchenette
tv	Television
ctv	Cable Television
pb	Private Bathroom
sb	Shared Bathroom
bkfst incl.	Breakfast Included
FAP	Full American Plan

HOTEL CLASSIFICATION

The prices in the guide are for one room, double occupancy in high season.

RESTAURANT CLASSIFICATION

$	less than $10
$$	$11 to $20
$$$	$21 to $30
$$$$	mmore than $31

The prices in the guide are for a meal for one person, not including drinks and tip.

All prices in this guide are in Canadian dollars.

Write to Us

The information contained in this guide was correct at press time. However, mistakes can slip in, omissions are always possible, places can disappear, etc. The authors and publisher hereby disclaim any liability for loss or damage resulting from omissions or errors.

We value your comments, corrections and suggestions, as they allow us to keep each guide up to date. The best contributions will be rewarded with a free book from Ulysses Travel Guides. All you have to do is write us at the following address and indicate which title you would be interested in receiving (see the list at the end of guide).

Ulysses Travel Guides
4176 Rue Saint-Denis
Montréal, Québec
Canada H2W 2M5
www.ulysses.ca
E-mail: text@ulysses.ca

Cataloguing

Canadian Cataloguing-in-Publication Data

Main entry under title:

Alberta's best hotels and restaurants
  (Ulysses travel guide)
  Includes index.
  ISBN 2-89464-304-7
  1. Tourist camps, hostels, etc. - Alberta - Guidebooks. 2. Hotels - Alberta - Guidebooks. 3. Restaurants - Alberta - Guidebooks. 4. Alberta - Guidebooks.
TX907.5.C22a42 2000   647.947123   C00-941738-9

Thanks

We acknowledge the financial support of the Government of Canada through the Book Publishing Industry Development Program (BPIDP) for our publishing activities.

We would also like to thank SODEC (Québec) for its financial support.

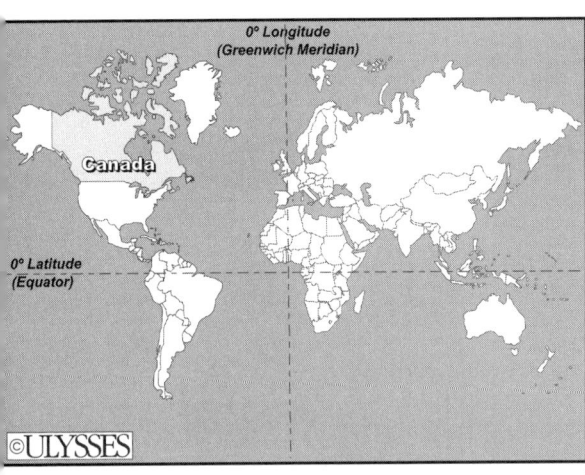

Where is Alberta?

Alberta
Capital: Edmonton
Population: 2,600,000 inhab.
Area: 661,000km² (255,200 sq mi)
Currency: Canadian Dollar

Alberta's Best Hotels and Restaurants

From towering mountains to wide-open heartlands, from concrete jungles to small farming towns, a journey through Alberta takes one to some surprisingly varied places.

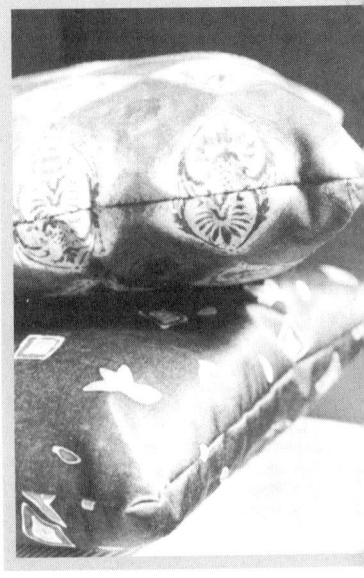

And whether closing a business deal in Calgary or looking for dinosaur bones in Drumheller, one thing is certain: the options for accommodation and food are just as varied as the terrain. That is where this guide comes in. It is designed to be a companion to your travels in Alberta, providing helpful advice on the best places to lay your head and satisfy your hunger.

A range of accommodations has been covered here, from major international hotels with all the comfort and service expected of them to rustic inns and lodges. You will find suggestions for accommodation in every region and corner of the province. All those listed here have been chosen because they offer excellent quality for the price.

The restaurants appearing in the guide have also been selected for their high-quality and value. From Asian cuisine in Calgary's Chinatown to juicy Alberta steaks in the province's north, this guide will help you discover some of the fantastic cuisine the province has to offer.

Tourist Information

Alberta's provincial tourism office will gladly send you general information by mail. Alternatively, you can check them out on their Web site:

Travel Alberta
Box 2500
Edmonton, Alberta
T5J 2Z1
☎ *800-661-8888 (North America)*
☎ *(780) 427-4321 (outside North America)*
≠ *(780) 427-0867*
info@travelalberta.com
www.travelalberta.com

Should you require more detailed information on a specific region of Alberta, contact the following offices of the Alberta Tourism Destination Regions:

Rocky Mountains
P.O. Box 1298
Banff, T0L 0C0
☎ *(403) 762-0279*

Calgary
C/O C.C.V.B.
200-237 8th Ave. SE
Calgary, T2G 0K8
☎ *800-661-1678*

Southern Alberta
2805 Scenic Dr.
Lethbridge
☎ *(403) 320-1222*
☎ *800-661-1222*

Central Alberta
☎ *(403) 346-5081*
☎ *800-215-8946*

Edmonton
9797 Jasper Ave.
Pedway Level
Edmonton, T5J 1N9
☎ *800-463-4667*

Northern Alberta
Box 1518
Slave Lake, T0G 2A0
☎ *(780) 849-6050*
☎ *800-756-4351*

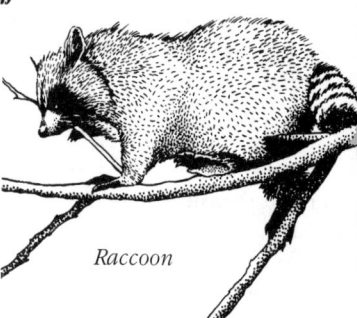

Raccoon

Telephone Calls

There are two area codes in Alberta:

403 for Calgary and southern Alberta;

780 for Edmonton, central and northern Alberta.

For maximum clarity, we have included the area code with each telephone and fax number.

Accommodations

A wide choice of types of accommodation to fit every budget is available in most regions of Alberta. Most places are very comfortable and offer a number of services.

Prices vary according to the type of accommodation. The lodging included herin generally offer a good quality/price ratio A credit card will make reserving a room much easier, since in many cases payment for the first night is required.

Many hotels offer corporate discounts as well as discounts for automobile club (CAA, AAA) members. Be sure to ask about these special rates as they are generally very easy to obtain. Furthermore, check in the travel brochures given out at tourist offices as there are often coupons inside.

Hotels

Hotels rooms abound, ranging from the modest to the luxurious. Most hotel rooms come equipped with a private bathroom. There are several internationally reputed hotels in Alberta, including several beauties in the Canadian Pacific chain.

Inns

Often set up in beautiful historic houses, inns offer quality lodging. There are a lot of these establishments which are more charming and usually more picturesque than hotels. Many are furnished with beautiful period pieces. Breakfast is often included.

Bed and Breakfasts

Unlike hotels or inns, rooms in private homes are not always equipped with a private bathroom. There are bed and breakfasts throughout Alberta, in the country as well as the city. They are generally advantageously priced, welcoming, and offer a homey, family atmosphere. Credit cards are not always accepted in bed and breakfasts.

Motels

There are many motels throughout the province, and though they tend to be cheaper, they often lack atmosphere. These are particularly useful when pressed for time.

Restaurants

There are excellent restaurants throughout Alberta. The local specialty is, without a doubt, Alberta beef. Most cities have a wide range of choices for all budgets, from fast food to fine dining.

Prices in this guide are for a meal for one person, excluding drinks and tip.

$	*$10 and less*
$$	*$11 to $20*
$$$	*$21 to $30*
$$$$	*$31 and more*

These prices are generally based on the cost of the evening meal; remember that lunch is considerably less expensive.

The legal drinking age is 18 in Alberta; if you're close to that age, expect to be asked for proof.

Taxes

Unless otherwise indicated, hotel rates and menu prices do not include tax. Both are subject to the federal Goods and Services tax (GST) of 7%. Alberta has no provincial sales tax but it does charge a 5% lodging tax on top of the nightly rate.

Tax Refunds for Non-Residents

Non-residents of Canada can obtain refunds for the GST paid on accommodations and goods purchased while in Canada. To obtain a refund, it is important to keep your receipts. Refunds of up to $500 are obtained by filling out and mailing a special form to Revenue Canada. Forms are available at airports and duty-free shops or by calling one of the following numbers:

☎ *800-66-VISIT or 800-668-4748 from within Canada*
☎ *(902) 432-5608 from outside Canada*

Tipping

In general, tipping applies to all table service: restaurants, bars and nightclubs (therefore no tipping in fast-food restaurants).

Alberta's Best Hotels and Restaurants   13

Servers in restaurants are usually tipped about 15% of the bill before taxes, but the amount varies, of course depending on the quality of service.

Chambermaids are tipped about $2 per day.

Valets are generally tipped $1 to $2 and **bellhops** get $1 per bag.

How To Use This Guide

Each chapter in this guide corresponds to a tourist region in Alberta. Hotels and restaurants are described for each town or area covered, with symbols that will allow you to differentiate them. The order is determined by cost, from least to most expensive.

Porcupine

Table of Distances (km/mi)
Via the shortest route

	Banff (AB)
Calgary (AB)	130/81
Campbell River (BC)	281/174 1068/662
Edmonton (AB)	1477/916 278/172 408/253
Fort St. John (BC)	655/406 1456/903 1290/800 881/546
Grande Prairie (AB)	207/128 1636/1014 1470/911 674/418
Jasper (AB)	395/245 603/374 1240/769 1075/666 278/172
Kamloops (BC)	661/410 1057/655 970/601 579/359 413/256 489/303
Lethbridge (AB)	843/523 632/392 949/557 1157/717 1422/882 1256/779 354/219
Medicine Hat (AB)	165/102 906/562 695/431 1012/627 1219/756 1485/921 1319/818 416/258
Penticton (BC)	967/600 904/560 247/153 567/352 1118/693 1189/737 446/277 481/298 550/341
Prince George (BC)	1070/663 1007/624 514/319 722/448 1139/737 455/282 740/459 959/595 481/298 650/405
Prince Rupert (BC)	733/454 1461/906 1741/1079 1242/770 374/232 542/336 1276/791 1474/914 1001/621 835/518 653/405
Red Deer (AB)	815/505 1804/1118 358/222 1108/687 232/135 1189/737 1474/914 708/439 989/613 1387/860
Vancouver (BC)	1652/1024 421/261 754/467 543/337 790/490 135/84 1334/827 1168/724 265/164
Victoria (BC)	1102/683 941/583 1253/777 347/215 1009/626 1404/870 361/224 1224/759 1245/772 233/144 967/600 836/518
	106/66 1168/724 989/613 835/518 1319/818 1256/779 413/256 1075/666 1470/911 1290/800 271/168 1311/813 1033/640 902/559

Example: The distance between Jasper (AB) and Penticton (BC) is 722km / 448mi.

Banff (AB)
Calgary (AB)
Campbell River (BC)
Edmonton (AB)
Fort St. John (BC)
Grande Prairie (AB)
Jasper (AB)
Kamloops (BC)
Lethbridge (AB)
Medicine Hat (AB)
Penticton (BC)
Prince George (BC)
Prince Rupert (BC)
Red Deer (AB)
Vancouver (BC)
Victoria (BC)

©ULYSSES

The Rocky Mountains

Breathtakingly beautiful, the Canadian Rockies stretch down the easternmost edge of British Columbia and western Alberta before plunging thousands of metres to meet the waving grasses of the prairies.

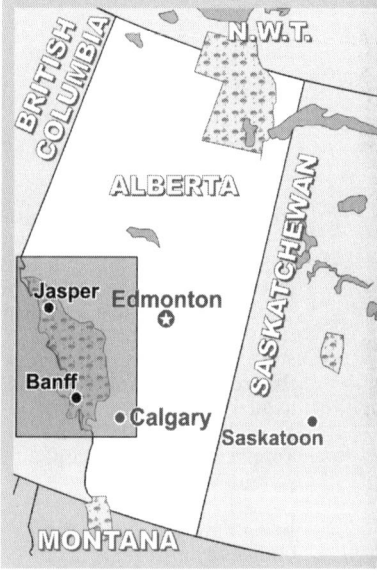

Born from a deep sea 600 million years ago along the Pacific tectonic plate and the North American continental plate, the 1,450km-chain (901mi) of craggy snow-capped peaks and deep forests matches the image that many visitors have of the Canadian wilderness. With its awe-inspiring panoramic views, it is little wonder the economy of the Rockies is now firmly centred around tourism.

Two major resort areas can be found here: Banff and Jasper. The town of Banff, situated in Banff National Park, is the more famous with charming store-fronted streets where elk and humans compete for space. It is also just a short drive from Lake Louise, a small town with the striking emerald-green lake of the same name and a view of the Victoria Glacier that attracts about six million visitors a year. Though equally beautiful, Jasper, at the northern end of Alberta's Rockies, is a quieter, somewhat less popular alternative.

The view from British Columbia's side of the mountains is also incredible with Kootenay and Yoho national parks as the main attractions.

Accommodations

In the summer, the region's resort towns are teeming with tourists. As a result, prices at Banff's seemingly countless hotels are almost double that of the off-season. A list of private homes that receive paying guests is available. It can be obtained from the **Banff-Lake Louise Tourist Office** at 224 Banff Avenue.

In and around Banff, the choices vary from a wide number of campgrounds to the five-star Canadian Pacific Banff Springs Hotel along with everything else in between. Lake Louise also has a large number of hotels, the most famous being the Chateau Lake Louise with its incredible view of the lake and glacier. Unfortunately, the picturesque setting does not come at a low price, but there are more reasonable options available in the town.

While extremely busy and the streets of Jasper lack the bustling hordes of tourists to be found in Banff, the natural environment is just as majestic. The town also has its share of high-end accommodations, but there are some more reasonably priced inns and lodges to be found.

Kootenay and Yoho national parks in British Columbia are less frequented than Banff and Jasper, but really should not be missed. The landscapes are breathtaking and accommodations are much cheaper.

Kananaskis Country, a beautiful area southwest of Banff, has become extremely popular as a weekend getaway for residents of Calgary. For accommodations, the town of Canmore is an obvious choice.

Restaurants

There is a wide range of restaurants throughout the region. As is the case with so many tourist hot spots, however, you don't always get the quality you pay for. Nevertheless, there are plenty of jewels to be found, including some

Restaurants

quality East Asian cuisine, a plethora of hearty Western-style restaurants and some excellent dining rooms. If it's steaks, burgers or pizza that you're looking for, you will have absolutely no trouble finding it. Other dining options are also readily available.

After dinner, take a stroll. The Rockies are even more inspiring at twilight.

Canmore

Alpine Club of Canada
$20-$35
4.5km east of Canmore on Hwy. 1A
☎ *(403) 678-3200*
≠ *(403) 678-3224*

The Alpine Club of Canada offers an interesting alternative for nature lovers who want to sleep "in the great outdoors." This association has huts not only near Canmore, but also in several areas of the Rocky Mountains. You can even combine hiking tours with accommodation in these huts.

Rundle Mountain Motel & Gasthaus
$63-$108
tv, ≈
1723 Mountain Ave.
Canmore, AB, T1W 1L7
☎ *(403) 678-5322*
☎ *800-661-1610*
≠ *(403) 678-5813*

Rundle Mountain Motel & Gasthaus is a motel modelled on Savoy-style chalets. It has 51 rooms that are in keeping with this type of establishment.

Ambleside Lodge
$65-$105
non-smokers only
123A Rundle Dr.
Canmore, AB, T1W 2L6
☎ *(403) 678-3976*
≠ *(403) 678-3916*

Ambleside Lodge welcomes you to a large and handsome residence in the style of a Savoyard chalet just a few minutes from the centre of town. The big and friendly common room is graced with a beautiful fireplace. Some rooms have private baths.

Cougar Canyon B&B
$65-$90
3 Canyon Rd., Box 3515
Canmore, AB, T0L 0M0
☎ *(403) 678-6636*
≠ *(403) 3293*

Cougar Canyon B&B has two second-floor guest rooms each with an *en suite* full bath. One of the rooms has a queen-size bed, the other two twin beds. Adjoining these rooms, a loft features panoramic views, a fireplace, a television, a VCR, and a small library. Guests join hosts for breakfast in a main-floor dining room with a double-sided fireplace which is very cozy in winter. Full breakfasts start with fresh-squeezed orange juice and include home baking. There are hiking trails at the back

floor, while four world-class golf courses and five ski hills are within a one-hour drive. Cross-country skiing and mountain biking can be enjoyed across town at Canmore Nordic Centre. English and German spoken.

Best Western Green Gables Inn
$79-$139
≈, ℜ, tv, ☺, ®
1602 2nd Ave. (Hwy 1A)
Canmore, AB, T1W 1M8
☎ *(403) 678-5488*
☎ *800-661-2133*
≠ *(403) 678-2670*

To reach the Best Western Green Gables Inn, take the Canmore exit from the highway and follow Highway 1A. This Best Western hotel has plenty of charm. The rooms are particularly spacious and tastefully decorated in very warm tones.

Lady MacDonald Country Inn
$80-$175
⊂, tv
Bow Valley Trail, Box 2128
Canmore, AB, T0L 0M0
☎ *(403) 678-3665*
☎ *800-567-3919*
≠ *(403) 678-9714*

Lady MacDonald Country Inn is a magnificent little inn established in a very pretty house. Eleven elegantly decorated rooms are placed at guests' disposal. Some rooms have been specially equipped to receive disabled travellers; others are spread over two floors to welcome families of four. The superb "Three Sisters Room" offers a magnificent view of the Rundle Range and Three Sisters mountains, as well as a fireplace and a whirlpool bath.

Georgetown Inn
$89-$169 bkfst incl.
⊂, tv, ℜ
1101 Bow Valley Trail
Canmore, AB, T1W 1N4
☎ *(403) 678-3439*
≠ *(403) 678-6909*

Georgetown Inn has resolutely gone for an old-fashioned British ambiance. Rooms are comfortable, and some are equipped with whirlpool baths. Breakfast, served in the Three Sisters dining room, is included in the price of your room. The fireplace, the old books and the reproductions hung on the walls give this place a warm atmosphere.

Rocky Mountain Ski Lodge
$100-$220
K, tv
1711 Mountain Ave., Box 8070
Canmore, AB, T1W 2T8
☎ *(403) 678-5445*
☎ *800-665-6111*
≠ *(403) 678-6484*

Rocky Mountain Ski Lodge faces a pleasant little garden. Rooms are clean and spacious. Units with livingrooms, fireplaces, and fully equipped kitchens start at $120.

The Creek House
**$195 or
$2,100- $2,800/week for 4 people**
701 Mallard Alley
Canmore, AB, T1W 2A8
☎ *(403) 678-2463*
☎ *888-678-6100*
≈ *(403) 678-8721*
www.creekhouse.com

The Creek House is one of the most beautiful places to spend the night in Canmore and all of the Rockies. Gail and Greg bought and completely renovated this old house on the edge of the Bow River from where you can see Cascade Mountain (3,000m or 9,843 ft). The decor in the rooms is impeccable. An artist made some magnificent murals, such as the one in the stairwell. At the end of 1999, Greg added the final touch – a rooftop jacuzzi!

Boston Pizza
$
every day from 11am
1704 Bow Valley Trail
☎ *(403) 678-3300*

Boston Pizza falls into the fast-food category. This restaurant serves a wide variety of pizzas, nachos and big sandwiches.

The Kabin
$
every day
1712 Hwy. 1A
☎ *(403) 678-4878*

The Kabin offers copious breakfasts, as well as lunches and suppers, in a restored old wooden house. In warm weather, you can eat on the terrace.

Nutter's
$
every day
900 Railway Ave.
☎ *(403) 678-3335*

Nutter's is the best spot to find the fixings for sandwiches or other snacks for your back-country hikes. You will find a large selection of energizing or natural foods to take out, or you can eat in at the small tables near the windows.

Santa Lucia
$
closed Sun
714 8th St.
☎ *(403) 678-3414*

Santa Lucia is a small Italian restaurant with a family atmosphere. The *gnocchis* are excellent. They also deliver.

Beaver

✕ Chez François
$$
adjacent to the Best Western
Green Gables Inn
Hwy 1A
☎ *(403) 678-6111*

Chez François is probably the best place to eat in Canmore. The chef, who comes from Québec, offers excellent French cuisine and a warm atmosphere in his restaurant.

✕ Peppermill
$$
726 9th St.
☎ *(403) 678-2292*

Peppermill is a good little 12-table restaurant with a traditional menu. The house specialty is pepper steak. The Swiss chef will happily serve a delicious *fendant du Valais* (Swiss white wine). Reservations are recommended.

✕ Sinclairs
$$
every day
637 8th St.
☎ *(403) 678-5370*

Sinclairs offers good food in a warm ambiance enhanced by a fireplace. Reservations are recommended in high season, when the restaurant is often full. It also offers an excellent selection of teas, a rarity around here.

Banff and Surroundings

Norquay's Timberline Inn
$64-$143 for rooms
$160-$285 for cabins
a little before the entrance to Banff
north of the Trans-Canada Hwy.
and near Mount Norquay
Box 69, Banff, AB, T0L 0C0
☎ *(403) 762-2281*
≠ *(403) 762-8331*

Norquay's Timberline Inn offers views of Mount Norquay from its lower-priced rooms, and views of the valley and city of Banff from the others. Though the higher-priced rooms have prettier views, they do unfortunately also overlook the Trans-Canada. There are two very peaceful cabins available on the Mount Norquay side in the middle of the forest; one for six people and the other for four. This establishment plans to completely renovate its rooms in 2000-2001.

Red Carpet Inn
$65-$150
≡, ⊛, *tv*
425 Banff Ave.
☎ *762-4184 or 800-563-4609*
≠ *762-4694*

Recently renovated, the Red Carpet Inn offers simply decorated, lovely rooms. Enjoy a good night's sleep on the soft mattresses.

Holiday Lodge
$67 bkfst incl.
311 Marten St.
Box 904, Banff, AB, T0L 0C0
☎ *(403) 762-3648*
≠ *762-8813*

Holiday Lodge has five clean and relatively comfortable rooms and two cabins. This old restored house, located in the centre of town, offers good and copious breakfasts.

Homestead Inn
$70-$130
tv
217 Lynx St.
☎ *762-4471 or 800-661-1021*
≠ *762-8877*

The Homestead Inn is located in the heart of Banff, but not on busy Banff Avenue which is an advantage in itself. Tastefully decorated rooms and large beds.

King Edward Hotel
$75-$150
tv
137 Banff Ave.
☎ *(403) 462-2202*
☎ *800-344-4232*
≠ *(403) 762-0876*

The King Edward Hotel is one of the largest buildings in town. Though it had a complete facelift a while ago, it has kept its old-world charm. The attentive staff makes for a pleasant stay.

ACCOMMODATIONS

1. Banff Rocky Mountain Resort
2. Banff Springs Hotel
3. Banff Voyager Inn
4. Bow View Motor Lodge
5. Brewster's Mountain Lodge
6. Caribou Lodge
7. Douglas Fir Resort & Chalets
8. High Country Inn
9. Holiday Lodge
10. Homestead Inn
11. Inns of Banff, Swiss Village and Rundle Manor
12. King Edward Hotel
13. Mount Royal Hotel
14. Norquay's Timberline Inn
15. Red Carpet Inn
16. Rimrock Resort Hotel
17. Rundle Stone Lodge
18. Tannenhof Pension
19. Traveller's Inn
20. Tunnel Mountain Chalets

RESTAURANTS

1. Athena Pizza
2. Balkan Restaurant
3. Cabouse
4. Grizzly House
5. Joe BTFSPLK's
6. Korean Restaurant
7. Le Beaujolais
8. Magpie & Stump
9. Rose and Crown
10. Silver Dragon Restaurant
11. Sukiyaki House
12. The Cake Company
13. Ticino

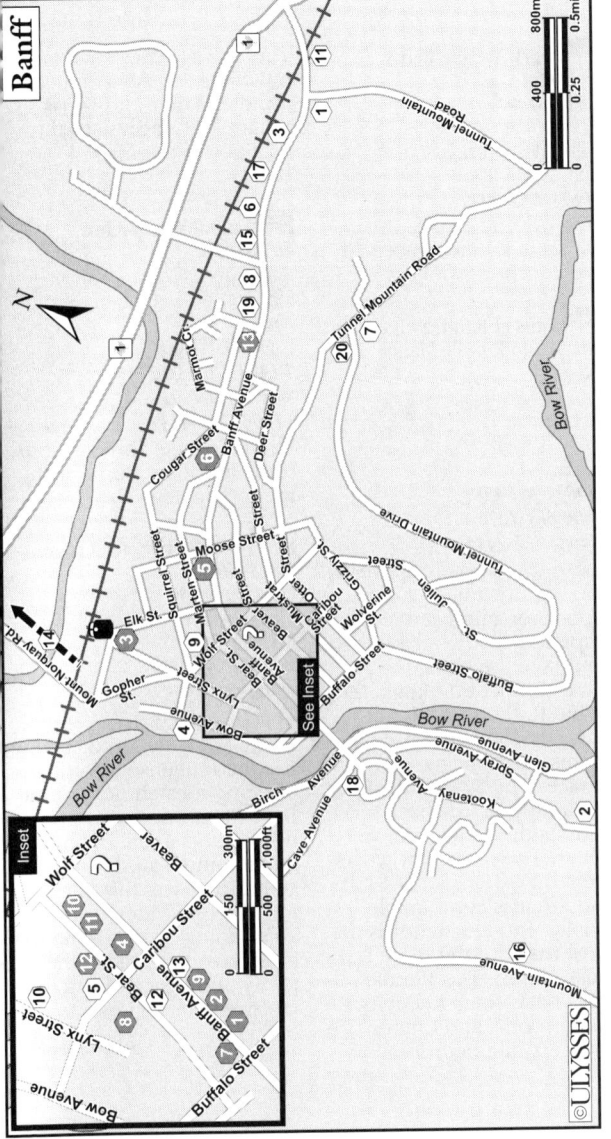

Park Avenue Bed & Breakfast
$75 bkfst incl.
no credit cards
135B Park Ave., Box 783
Banff, AB, T0L 0C0
☎*(403) 762-2025*

Park Avenue Bed & Breakfast rents two rooms exclusively to non-smokers.

Inns of Banff, Swiss Village and Rundle Manor
$80-$215
tv
600 Banff Ave.
Box 1077, Banff
AB, T0L 0C0
☎*(403) 762-4581*
☎*800-661-1272*
≠*(403) 762-2434*

These three hotels are really one big hotel with a common reservation service. Depending on your budget, you have the choice of three distinct buildings. Inns of Banff, the most luxurious, has 180 very spacious rooms, each facing a small terrace. The Swiss Village has a little more character and fits the setting much better. The rooms, however are a bit expensive at $150 and are less comfortable. Finally, Rundle Manor is the most rustic of the three but lacks charm. The Rundle's units have small kitchens, living rooms and one or two separate bedrooms. This is a safe bet for family travellers. Guests at the Rundle Manor and Swiss Village have access to the facilities of the Inns of Banff.

Banff Voyager Inn
$85-$140
⊛, *tv*, △, ≈, ℜ
555 Banff Ave.
Box 1540
Banff, AB, T0L 0C0
☎*(403) 762-3301*
☎*800-879-1991*
≠*(403) 762-4131*

Banff Voyager Inn has comfortable rooms, some with mountain views.

Bow View Motor Lodge
$90-$150
♿, ⊛, *tv*, ≈, ℜ
228 Bow Ave., Box 339
Banff, AB, T0L 0C0
☎*(403) 762-2261*
☎*800-661-1565*
≠*(403) 762-8093*

The Bow View Motor Lodge has the immense advantage of being located next to the Bow River and far from noisy Banff Avenue. Only a five minute walk from the centre of town, this charming hotel provides comfortable rooms; those facing the river have balconies. The pretty and peaceful restaurant welcomes guests for breakfast.

Banff and Surroundings 25

Rundle Stone Lodge
$95-$190
&, P, tv, ≈, ⊛
537 Banff Ave., Box 489
Banff, AB, T0L 0C0
☎*(403) 762-2201*
☎*800-661-8630*
≈*(403) 762-4501*

Rundle Stone Lodge occupies a handsome building along Banff's main street. In the part of the building located along Banff Avenue, the rooms are attractive and spacious, each with a balcony. Some also have whirlpool baths. The hotel offers its guests a covered, heated parking area in the winter. Rooms for disabled travellers are available on the ground floor.

Tannanhof Pension
$95-$165 bkfst incl.
✖
121 Cave Ave., Box 1914
Banff, AB, T0L 0C0
☎*(403) 762-4636*
≈*(403) 760-2484*

Tannanhof Pension has eight rooms and two suites located in a lovely, big house. Some rooms have cable television and private baths, while others share a bathroom. Each of the two suites has a bathroom with tub and shower, a fireplace and a sofa-bed for two extra people. Breakfast is German-style with a choice of four dishes.

Traveller's Inn
$95-$195
&, P, tv, △, ⊛
401 Banff Ave., Box 1017
Banff, AB, T0L 0C0
☎*(403) 762-4401*
☎*800-661-0227*
≈*(403) 762-5905*

Most rooms at the hotel have small balconies that offer fine mountain views. Rooms are simply decorated, big and cozy. The hotel has a small restaurant that serves breakfast, as well as heated underground parking, an advantage in the winter. During the ski season, guests have the use of lockers for skis and boots as well as a small store for the rental and repair of winter sports equipment.

Caribou Lodge
$100-$190
&, ⊛, tv, ℜ, △, ⊘
521 Banff Ave., Box 279
Banff, AB, T0L 0C0
☎*(403) 762-5887*
☎*800-563-8764*
≈*(403) 762-5918*

Caribou Lodge is another Banff Avenue hotel offering comfortable, spacious rooms. A rustic western decor of varnished wood characterizes the reception area and guest rooms. The restaurant at the Caribou Lodge, **The Keg**, serves American breakfasts and buffet-style food.

The Rocky Mountains

Ptarmigan Inn
$100-$200
⊛, △, ≡, ℜ, *tv*
337 Banff Ave
☎ *(403) 762-2207*
☎ *800-661-8310*
≠ *(403) 762-3577*

The Ptarmigan Inn reopened its doors in February 1999 after several million dollars' worth of renovations. They have made the place more attractive, especially the natural wood that adds charm to its 134 rooms.

Caribou

Douglas Fir Resort & Chalets
$120-$200
≡, ⊛, △, ≡, K, *tv*
525 Tunnel Mountain Road
☎ *762-5591 or 800-661-9267*
≠ *762-8774*
www.douglasfir.com

The recently renovated Douglas Fir Resort & Chalets has 133 rooms and fully equipped cottages (fridge, stove, fireplace) that are ideal for families. Their pleasant layout makes them feel like apartments. Besides offering an incredible view of Mount Rundle, you can take advantage of the squash courts, pool and indoor waterslides.

High Country Inn
$125
△, P, *tv*, ≈, ⊛
419 Banff Ave., Box 700
Banff, AB T0L 0C0
☎ *(403) 762-2236*
☎ *800-661-1244*
≠ *(403) 762-5084*

Located on Banff's main drag, this inn has big, comfortable, spacious rooms with balconies. Furnishings are very ordinary, however, and detract from the beauty of the setting.

Banff Rocky Mountain Resort
$150-$230
tv, ⊛, ≈, ☺
squash courts, massage room, tennis courts
at the entrance to the town along Banff Ave.
Box 100, Banff, AB T0L 0C0
☎ *(403) 762-5531*
☎ *800-661-9563*
≠ *(403) 762-5166*

Banff Rocky Mountain Resort is an ideal spot if you are travelling as a family in Banff National Park. The delightful little chalets are warm and very well equipped. On the ground floor is a bathroom with shower, a very functional kitchen facing a living room and dining room with a fireplace while upstairs are two bedrooms and another bathroom. These apartments also have small private terraces. Near the main building are picnic and barbecue areas as well as lounge chairs where you can lie in the sun.

Brewster's Mountain Lodge
$200-$400

⊛, ⌂, tv
208 Caribou St.
Box 2286 T0L 0C0
☎ *(403) 762-5454*
☎ *800-691-5085*
≠ *(403) 762-3953*

Brewster's Mountain Lodge features spacious rooms with a mountain decor including cozy log furniture. It is centrally located and a good place to organize your trip from since they offer many touring options.

Tunnel Mountain Chalets
$220-$280 per chalet

⊛, ⌂, ≈, tv, K
intersection of Tunnel Mountain Rd. and Tunnel Mountain Dr.
Box 1137 T0L 0C0
☎ *(403) 762-4515*
☎ *800-661-1859*
≠ *(403) 762-5183*

Tunnel Mountain Chalets offers fully-equipped cottages and condo-style units with kitchens, fireplaces and patios. This is a great option for families and for those looking to save some money by avoiding eating out. The interiors are standard, but clean and very comfortable. The larger units can sleep up to eight people.

Rimrock Resort Hotel
$225-$1,200

⊛, ≡, ℜ, ≈, ⌂, tv
100 Mountain Ave.
Box 1110 T0L 0C0
☎ *(403) 762-3365*
☎ *800-661-1587*
≠ *(403) 762-4132*

From afar, the Rimrock Resort Hotel stands out majestically from the mountainside much like the Banff Springs does. The rooms are equally well appointed though more modern. The various categories of rooms are based on the views that they offer; the best view is of the Bow and Spray Valleys *($335)*. The hotel is right across the street from the Upper Hot Springs.

Banff Springs Hotel
$240-$520

⊛, ⊘, ≈, ⌂, ⚘, ✈, tv, ℜ, ≈, bar
Spray Ave., Box 960
Banff, AB T0L 0C0
☎ *(403) 762-2211*
☎ *800-441-1414*
≠ *762-4447*

Banff Springs Hotel is the biggest hotel in Banff. Overlooking the town, this five-star hotel, part of the Canadian Pacific chain, offers 770 luxurious rooms in an atmosphere reminiscent of an old Scottish castle. The hotel was designed by architect Bruce Price, to whom is also credited Windsor Station in Montréal and the Château Frontenac in Québec City. Besides typical turn-of-the-century chateau style, old-fashioned furnishings and superb views from every window, the hotel offers its guests bowling, tennis courts, a pool, a sauna, a large whirlpool bath, and a massage room. You can also stroll and shop in the more than 50 shops in the hotel. Golfers will be delighted to find a superb 27-hole course, designed by architect Stanley Thompson, on the grounds.

Mount Royal Hotel
$250
tv, bar, ⊛, ☺, ℜ
billiards room
138 Banff Ave., Box 550
Banff, AB T0L 0C0
☎ *(403) 762-3331*
☎ *800-267-3035*
⇌ *(403) 762-8938*

Mount Royal Hotel, right in the centre of town not far from the tourist information centre, rents comfortable rooms.

The Cake Company
$
every day
218 Bear St.
☎ *(403) 762-2230*

The Cake Company is a little tea room that is ideal for a hot drink and a delicious slice of home-made cake.

Joe BTFSPLK's
$
221 Banff Ave.
facing the tourist information centre
☎ *(403) 762-5529*

Joe BTFSPLK's (pronounced bi-tif-spliks) is a small restaurant with 1950s decor and good hamburgers. You'll learn that Joe BTFSPLK was a strange comic book character who walked around with a cloud above his head causing disasters wherever he went. It seems the only way today to avoid annoyances (such as spending too much money) may be to come to this little restaurant, very popular with locals for the burgers, fries, salads, chicken fingers and milkshakes. The restaurant also serves breakfasts for under $6.

Rose and Crown
$
every day 11am to 2am
upstairs at 202 Banff Ave.
☎ *(403) 762-2121*

Rose and Crown prepares light meals consisting essentially of hamburgers, chicken wings and *nachos*. In the evening, the spot becomes a bar with musicians.

Banff and Surroundings 29

✕ Silver Dragon Restaurant
$
every day 11:30am to 11pm
211 Banff Ave.
☎(403) 762-3939
Silver Dragon Restaurant offers adequate Chinese cuisine. They also deliver.

✕ Athena Pizza
$$
every day
112 Banff Ave.
☎(403) 762-4022 or 762-2022
Athena Pizza cooks up pizzas in its oven after topping them with a ton of ingredients. Tasty pizza made to order.

✕ Balkan Restaurant
$$
every day 11am to 11pm
120 Banff Ave.
☎(403) 762-3454
Balkan Restaurant is Banff's Greek restaurant. With fake vines and grape clusters the blue and white decor recalls the Mediterranean. The main dishes are good, although they are unimaginative and often show North American influences. The staff seems overworked and are not always very pleasant.

✕ Grizzly House
$$
every day 11:30am to midnight
207 Banff Ave.
☎(403) 762-4055
Grizzly House specializes in big, tender, juicy steaks. The western decor is a bit corny, but your attention will quickly be diverted by your delicious meal.

 ✕ Korean Restaurant
$$
every day from 11:30am to 10pm
upstairs at Cascade Plaza
317 Banff Ave.
☎(403) 762-8862
For anyone who has never tried Korean cuisine, here is a good chance to discover fine, deliciously prepared food. The staff will be happy to advise you in your selections.

✕ Magpie & Stump
$$
203 Cariboo St.
☎(403) 762-4067
Magpie & Stump serves Mexican dishes accompanied with refried beans, Spanish rice, salads, sour cream and salsa. Its classy decor gives it a distinguished ambience.

The Rocky Mountains

Sukiyaki House
$$
every day
upstairs at 211 Banff Ave.
☎ *(403) 762-2002*
Sukiyaki House offers excellent Japanese cuisine at affordable prices. The sushi is perfect, and the staff is very courteous. The impersonal decor, however, leaves a bit to be desired.

Ticino
$$
5:30pm to 10:30pm
415 Banff Ave.
☎ *(403) 762-3848*
Ticino serves pretty good Italian cuisine as well as fondues. The decor is very ordinary, and the music tends to be too loud.

Caboose
$$$
every day 5pm to 10pm
corner of Elk St. and Lynx St.
☎ *(403) 762-3622*
☎ *762-2102*
Caboose is one of Banff's better eateries. The fish dishes, trout or salmon, are excellent, or you may prefer the lobster with steak, American style, or perhaps the crab. This is a favourite with regular visitors.

Le Beaujolais
$$$$
every day
212 Buffalo St.
☎ *(403) 762-2712*
Le Beaujolais prepares excellent French cuisine. The dining room is very elegant and the staff is highly attentive. British Columbia salmon, baked with Pernod, is a true delicacy. The best food in Banff.

Between Banff and Lake Louise

Johnston Canyon Resort
$98-$240
vcr, ✄, pb
from Banff, take the Trans-Canada Hwy to the Bow Valley exit then take Hwy 1A
the Bow Valley Parkway
Box 875, Banff, AB T0L 0C0
☎ *(403) 762-2971*
≈ *(403) 762-0868*
Johnston Canyon Resort constitutes a group of small log cabins right in the middle of the forest. The absolute calm is suitable for retreats. Some cabins offer a basic level of comfort, while others are fully equipped and have kitchens, sitting rooms and fireplaces. The biggest cabin can accommodate four people comfortably. A small grocery store, offering a basic range of products, is part of this tourism complex.

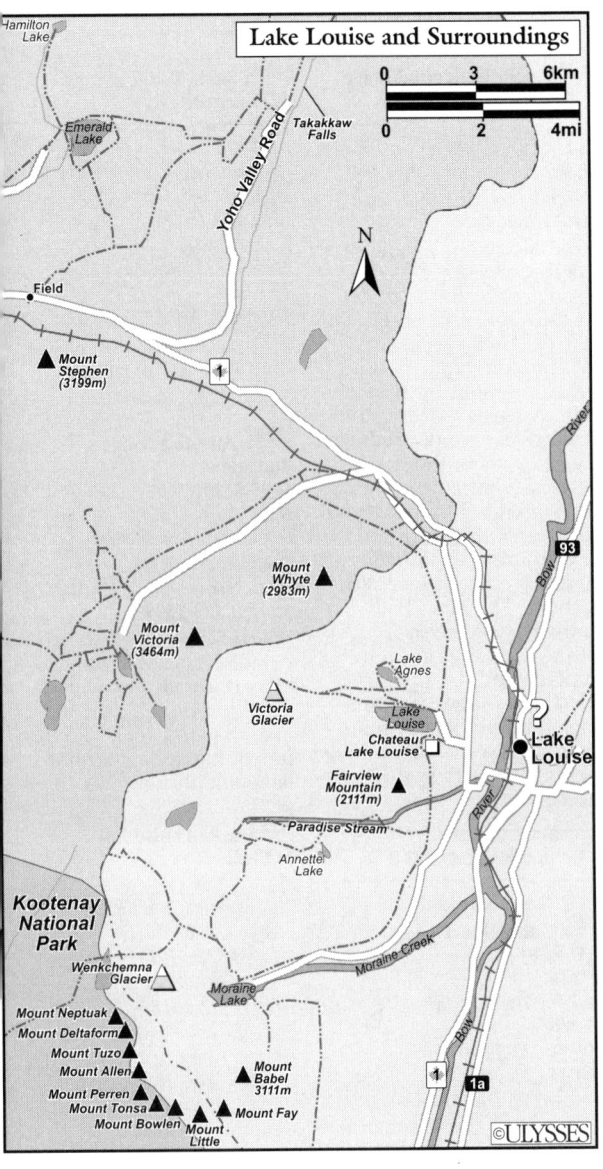

Castle Mountain Village
$190-$210
tv, K
Box 178, Lake Louise, AB
T0L 1E0
☎ *(403) 522-2783*
☎ *(403) 762-3868*

Castle Mountain Village is a superb collection of 19 small log cabins located at Castle Junction on Highway 1A. Each cabin can accommodate four people, with some housing up to eight. A small grocery store provides everyday products. The interiors of the cabins are very comfortable and seem intended to make you feel at ease. Kitchens are fully equipped and include microwave ovens and dishwashers. The main bathrooms have whirlpool baths. A roaring fire in the fireplace and the VCRs provided in the newer cabins constitute the perfect remedy for those cold mountain evenings. A very good choice.

Lake Louise

Mountaineer Lodge
$100-$240
△, ⚿, *tv*, ⊛
Box 150, Lake Louise, AB
T0L 1E0
☎ *(403) 522-3844*
≠ *(403) 522-3902*

Located in the village of Lake Louise, the Mountaineer Lodge has 78 rather simply furnished rooms.

Skoki Lodge
$131 per person fb
open mid-Dec to Apr and Jun to Sep
△, *outhouse*
reached by an 11-km trail (hike, ride, or ski) from the Lake Louise ski slopes
Box 5, Lake Louise, AB
T0L 1E0
☎ *(403) 522-3555*

All meals are included in the price of the room.

Paradise Lodge & Bungalows
$135-$230
K, ⚿, *tv*, ℝ
on your right, just after the Lake Moraine cutoff
Box 7, Lake Louise, AB, T0L 1E0
☎ *(403) 522-3595*
≠ *(403) 522-3987*

Paradise Lodge & Bungalows is a complex with 21 small log bungalows and 24 luxury suites. It should be noted that rooms do not have telephones.

Lake Louise Inn
$143-$264
✘, *tv*, ≈, ℜ
210 Village Rd., Box 209
Lake Louise, AB, T0L 1E0
☎ *(403) 522-3791*
☎ *800-661-9237*
≠ *(403) 522-2018*

Lake Louise Inn is located in the village of Lake Louise. The hotel offers very comfortable, warmly decorated rooms.

Deer Lodge
$160-$210
ℜ, ⊛
near the lake
on the right before reaching
the Chateau Lake Louise
Box 100
Lake Louise, AB, T0L 1E0
☎ *(403) 522-3747*
≠ *(403) 522-3883*

Deer Lodge is a very handsome and comfortable hotel. While the rooms are spacious and tastefully decorated, the atmosphere is very pleasant. The restaurant *($$$)* is attractive with a somewhat rustic decor and serves excellent food.

Moraine Lake Lodge
$320-$395
ငြ, ℜ
Box 70
Lake Louise, AB, T0L 1E0
☎ *(403) 522-3733*
≠ *(403) 522-3719*
Jun to Sep
☎ *(250) 985-7456*
Oct to May
≠ *(250) 985-7479*

Moraine Lake Lodge is located at the edge of Lake Moraine. Rooms do not have phones or televisions. The setting is magnificent but packed with tourists at all times which detracts a bit from its tranquility. The restaurant *($$)* is a perfect place to enjoy good meals while contemplating the superb view over the lake and the Ten Peaks which stretch before your eyes.

Chateau Lake Louise
$329-$490
ငြ, *tv*, ≈, ℜ, △
Lake Louise, AB, T0L 1E0
☎ *(403) 522-3511*
≠ *(403) 522-3834*

Chateau Lake Louise is one of the best-known hotels in the region. Built originally in 1890, the hotel burned to the ground in 1892 and was rebuilt the following year. Another fire devastated parts of it in 1924. Since then, it has been expanded and embellished almost continuously. Today, this vast hotel, which belongs to the Canadian Pacific chain, has 511 rooms with space for more than 1,300 guests, and a staff of nearly 725 to look after your every need. Perched by the turquoise waters of Lake Louise, facing the Victoria Glacier, the hotel boasts a divine setting. The **Edelweiss Dining Room** *($$$)* offers delicious French cuisine in very elegant surroundings with a view over the lake. Reservations are recommended.

Post Hotel
$350-$520
tv, ≈, ℜ
Box 69, Lake Louise, AB
T0L 1E0
☎ *(403) 522-3989*
☎ *800-661-1586*
≠ *(403) 522-3966*

The magnificent Post Hotel is part of the Relais et Châteaux chain. Everything

The Rocky Mountains

at this elegant establishment, from the rooms to the grounds, is tastefully and carefully laid out. If you can afford the extra cost and are looking to treat yourself, then this is the best place in Lake Louise. The restaurant (*$$$*) is exquisite and the staff, friendly - making reservations a must.

Beeline Chicken & Pizza
$
every day
in Samson Mall
in the centre of Lake Louise village
☎(403) 522-2006
Beeline Chicken & Pizza prepares good hamburgers as well as pizzas, nachos and burritos.

Lake Louise Grill & Bar
$
every day
in Samson Mall
in the centre of Lake Louise village
☎(403) 522-3879
Lake Louise Grill & Bar serves Chinese food and traditional American cuisine in lacklustre fashion.

Icefields Parkway

The Crossing
$95
△, ℜ, tv, ⊛, *cafeteria, pub*
at the crossroads of Hwys 93 and 11, 80 km from Lake Louise
Box 333, Lake Louise, AB
T0L 1E0
☎(403) 761-7000
≈(403) 761-7006
The Crossing is a good place to stop along the Icefields Parkway and houses a fairly large and popular cafeteria (*$-$$*) which serves light meals.

Num-Ti-Jah Lodge
$125-$180
pb
on the shore of Bow Lake
about 35 km from Lake Louise
☎(403) 522-2167
≈(403) 522-2425
Num-Ti-Jah Lodge was built by Jimmy Simpson, a famous mountain guide and trapper from the region. His two daughters also have a place in the history of the Rockies. Peg and Mary became world-class figure skaters in their time and made numerous tours of Canada and the United States. The name Num-Ti-Jah comes from a Stoney Indian word for pine marten. As one of the most beautiful spots in the region, Bow Lake is popular

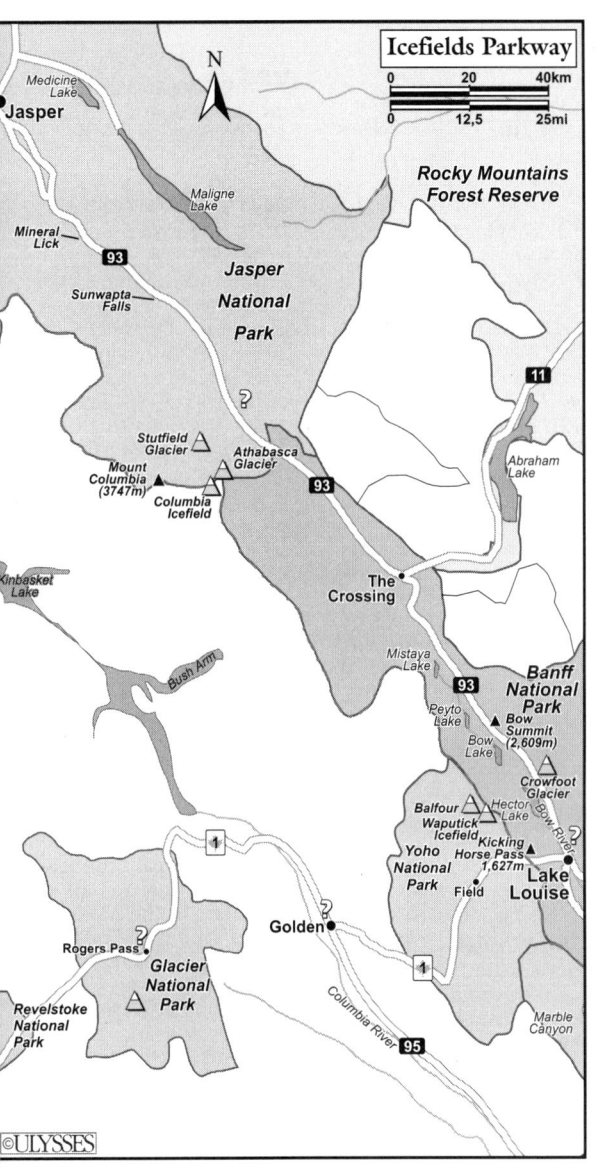

with tourists. Often crowded by the influx of tourists, the café *($)* serves sandwiches, muffins, and various hot beverages.

🛏 Columbia Icefield Chalet
$160-$200
open May to mid-Oct
ℜ, ♿, *pb*
Box 1140, Banff, T0L 0C0
Icefields Parkway
at the foot of the Athabasca Glacier
☎ *(403) 852-6550*
= *(403) 852-6568*
off-season ☎/= (403) 762-6735
The Columbia Icefield Chalet, with its terrifc location, boasts equally terrific views. If you can afford the extra $25, opt for the glacier-view rooms. All rooms are fairly standard with queen-sized beds and large bathrooms. You are staying here for the setting, after all.

Jasper

🛏 Skyline Accommodation
$30-$50
sb
726 Patricia St., Box 2616
Jasper, AB, T0E 1E0
☎ *(780) 852-5035*
Roger and Judy Smolnicky have renovated their big house to create three spacious guest rooms. The shared bath is very clean.

🛏 Private Accommodation at the Knauers'
$60 bkfst incl.
sb/pb, tv
708 Patricia St., Box 4
Jasper, AB, T0E 1E0
☎ *(780) 852-4916*
= *(780) 852-1143*
Private Accommodation at the Knauers' has three fairly large rooms that have the advantage of having their own private entrance. Two of the rooms, with rates set at $60, are next to a big and attractive bathroom, while the other has its own facilities. There is a refrigerator for guests at the entrance. This spot is for non-smokers, and pets are not admitted. Continental breakfast is served in the rooms.

🛏 Patricia Lake Bungalows
$65-$140
summer only
tv, K, ⊛
5km north by Patricia Lake Road
☎ *(780) 852-3560*
= *(780) 952-4060*
patlake@telusplanet.net
The Patricia Lake Bungalows are located in an idyllic setting in the mountains facing a pretty lake. The discreetly decorated individual bungalows are all cozy, while the kitchenettes make you feel at home. Just a stone's throw from outdoor activity areas.

Jasper

ACCOMMODATIONS

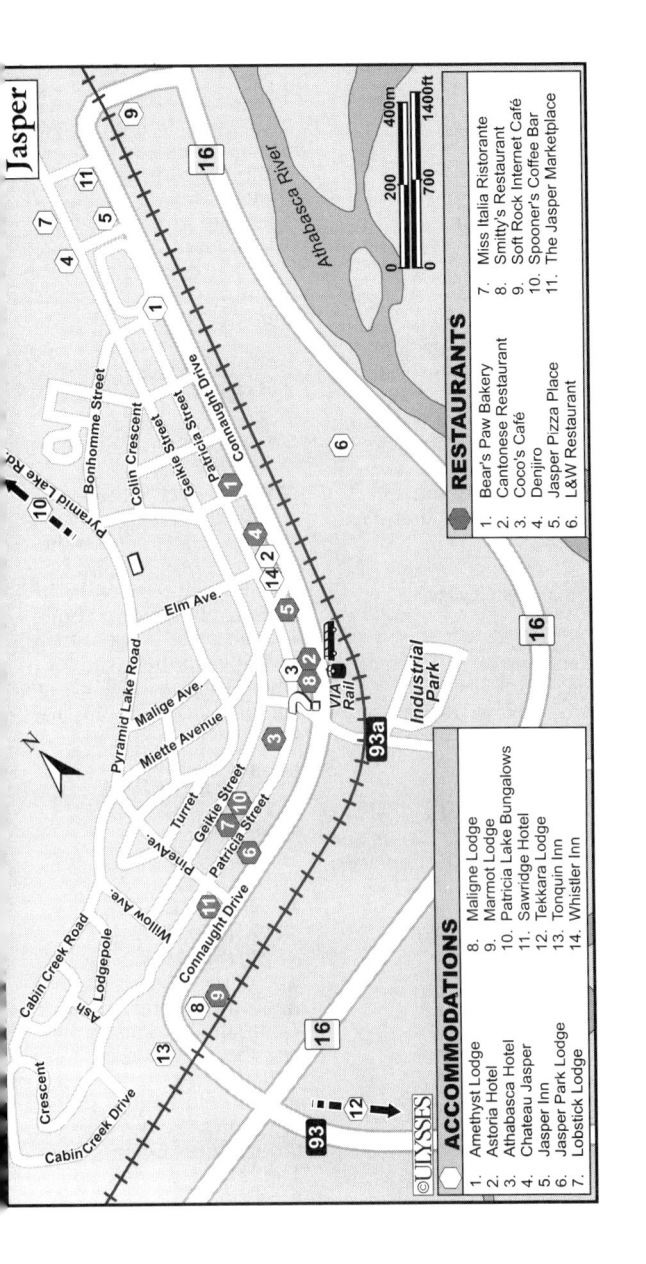

1. Amethyst Lodge
2. Astoria Hotel
3. Athabasca Hotel
4. Chateau Jasper
5. Jasper Inn
6. Jasper Park Lodge
7. Lobstick Lodge
8. Maligne Lodge
9. Marmot Lodge
10. Patricia Lake Bungalows
11. Sawridge Hotel
12. Tekkara Lodge
13. Tonquin Inn
14. Whistler Inn

RESTAURANTS

1. Bear's Paw Bakery
2. Cantonese Restaurant
3. Coco's Café
4. Denjiro
5. Jasper Pizza Place
6. L&W Restaurant
7. Miss Italia Ristorante
8. Smitty's Restaurant
9. Soft Rock Internet Café
10. Spooner's Coffee Bar
11. The Jasper Marketplace

© ULYSSES

Whistler Inn
$70-$268
tv, ℜ, △, P
Box 250, Jasper, AB, T0E 1E0
☎ *(780) 852-3361*
☎ *800-282-9919*
≠ *(780) 852-4993*

Renovations and upgrades have transformed the old Pyramid Hotel into the Whistler Inn. There is a steam room and an outdoor, rooftop hot tub. Each of the rooms, whose decor is standard but very tasteful, offers a view of the surroundings. Parking and ski lockers.

Maligne Lodge
$75-$164
≈, ✖, ♿, ℜ, △, ❋
on Connaught Dr.
leaving Jasper toward Banff
Box 757, Jasper, AB, T0E 1E0
☎ *(780) 852-3143*
☎ *800-661-1315*
≠ *(780) 852-4789*

Maligne Lodge offers 98 very comfortable rooms and suites, some with fireplaces and whirlpool baths.

Tonquin Inn
$79-$169
✖, ♿, tv, ≈, △, K, ℜ
on Connaught Dr.
at the entrance to Jasper
coming from Icefields Parkway
Box 658, Jasper, AB, T0E 1E0
☎ *(780) 852-4987*
☎ *800-661-1315*
≠ *(780) 852-4413*

The newer wing is laid out around the pool, providing all rooms direct access to it. The rooms in the old wing are less attractive and resemble motel rooms, though they do provide an adequate level of comfort. We suggest, nevertheless, that you request a room in the new wing when reserving your room.

Astoria Hotel
$80-$139
ℜ, tv
404 Connaught Dr.
☎ *(780) 852-3351*
☎ *800-661-7343*
≠ *(780) 852-5472*

The Astoria Hotel has the character and charm of a small European hotel. The attractively designed building faces the busiest street in Jasper in the centre of town. Built in 1920, it's one of the oldest building in Jasper.

Athabasca Hotel
$85-$135
sb/pb, ℜ, bar, tv
Box 1420, Jasper, AB
T0E 1E0
☎ *(780) 852-3386*
☎ *800-563-9859*
≠ *(780) 852-4955*

Athabasca Hotel is located right in the centre of Jasper, facing the Via Rail station and the Brewster and Greyhound bus terminal. Decorated in old English style, the rooms are not very big, though they are appealing. The least expensive are near a central bathroom, while the others have their own facilities. Neither flashy nor luxurious, this hotel is quite adequate, and the rooms are pleasant. This is the cheapest place to stay in Jasper, so you'll have to reserve in advance. The hotel does not have an elevator.

Marmot Lodge
$85-$170
≤, ✖, tv, ≈, ℜ, K, ⊛
on Connaught Dr.
at the Jasper exit, toward Edmonton
Box 1200, Jasper, AB, T0E 1E0
☎(780) 852-4471
☎800-661-6521
≠(780) 852-3280

Marmot Lodge offers very attractive rooms at what are considered reasonable prices in Jasper. The rooms are decorated in bright colours and old photographs hang on the walls, for a change from the normal decor. A terrace with tables has been set up in front of the pool, which is a good spot for sunbathing. The decor, the friendly staff and the scenery all contribute to making this hotel a very pleasant place. It provides the best quality-to-price ratio in town.

Jasper Inn
$96-$400
tv, ℜ, ≈, K, ⊛, ℝ
98 Geikie St., Box 879
Jasper, AB, T0E 1E0
☎(780) 852-4461
☎800-661-1933
≠(780) 852-5916

Jasper Inn offers spacious, attractive, comfortable rooms, some equipped with kitchenettes. The restaurant *($$)* is very popular, serving up excellent fish and seafood.

Amethyst Lodge
$119-$189
tv, ≡, ⊛
200 Connaught Dr.
☎(780) 852-3394 or 888-8JASPER
≠(780) 852-5198

Amethyst Lodge is a well-located, luxurious hotel whose exterior is not aesthetically pleasing, but its rooms are spacious and comfortable. The dining room *($$)* has been fully renovated and now offers its traditional menu in a pleasant atmosphere.

Lobstick Lodge
$119-$189
≡, ⊛, △, ℜ
96 Geikie St.
☎(780) 852-4431 or 888-8JASPER
≠(780) 852-4142

Lobstick Lodge is located some distance from town, but it's a fine, quality hotel.

🛏 ✕ Chateau Jasper
$128-$290
♿, ≈, ℛ, *heated parking*
Box 1418, Jasper, AB, T0E 1E0
☎ *(780) 852-5644*
☎ *800-661-9323*
⇌ *(780) 852-4860*

Chateau Jasper offers comfortable, very attractive rooms. Its restaurant, the **Beauvallon Dining Room** *($$$, ☎852-5644)*, prepares excellent French cuisine and is considered to be one of Jasper's finest dining establishments.

🏞 🛏 Tekkara Lodge
$139
K, ℑ
summer only
1km south of Jasper
☎ *(780) 852-3058*
⇌ *(780) 852-4636*

Tekkara Lodge is located in an idyllic spot near the banks of the Miette and Athabasca Rivers. The furnishing is luxurious and spacious, including fireplace and a kitchenette. Open your window and let yourself be lulled by the streams that flow down the glaciers in front of your door.

🏞 🛏 ✕ Jasper Park Lodge
$169-$419
♿, 🐾, ≈, ℛ, ℝ, *tv*, ☺, ⊛, △
Box 40, Jasper, AB, T0E 1E0
☎ *(780) 852-3301*
☎ *800-441-1414*
⇌ *(780) 852-5107*

Jasper Park Lodge constitutes beyond a doubt the most beautiful hotel complex in the whole Jasper area. Now part of the Canadian Pacific chain, the Jasper Park Lodge has attractive, spacious, comfortable rooms. It was built in 1921 by the Grand Trunk Railway Company to compete with Canadian Pacific's Banff Springs Hotel. The staff are very professional, attentive and friendly. A whole range of activities are organized for guests. These include horseback riding and river rafting. You will also find one of the finest golf courses in Canada, several tennis courts, a large pool, a sports centre, and canoes, sailboards and bicycles for rent in the summer, plus ski equipment in the winter. Several hiking trails criss-cross the site, among them a very pleasant 3.8km (2.4mi) trail alongside Lake Beauvert. Whether you're staying in a room in the main building or in a small chalet, you are assured of comfort and tranquility. Each year Jasper Park Lodge organizes theme events where hotel guests are invited to participate.

Some weekends may be dedicated to the mountains and relaxation, with yoga and aerobics classes as well as water gymnastics and visits to the sauna; while another weekend may be set aside for the wine tastings of Beaujolais Nouveau; other activities are organized for New Year's. Ask for the activities leaflet for more information. The **Beauvert Dining Room** *($$$)*, which offers mainly French Cuisine, is arguably the finest restaurant in Jasper.

Sawridge Hotel
$169-$229
&, *pub, tv,* ≈, ℜ, ⊛, △, *laundromat*
82 Connaught Dr., Box 2080
Jasper, AB, T0E 1E0
☎*(780) 852-5111*
☎*800-661-6427*
⇌*(780) 852-5942*
Sawridge Hotel offers big, warmly decorated rooms.

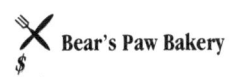

Bear's Paw Bakery
$
Cedar Ave.
near Connaught Dr.
☎*(780) 852-3233*
Bear's Paw Bakery makes buns and other treats at the crack of dawn. It also serves good coffee and juice. A good place for breakfast or a snack after hiking.

Coco's Café
$
every day
608 Patricia St.
☎*(780) 852-4550*
Coco's Café is a little spot that serves bagels, sandwiches and cheesecake.

Miss Italia Ristorante
$
every day
610 Patricia St.
upstairs at the Centre Mall
☎*(780) 852-4002*
Miss Italia Ristorante offers decent Italian cooking. The staff is friendly and attentive.

Smitty's Restaurant
$
near the tourist information centre
☎*(780) 852-3111*
Smitty's Restaurant may not look like much but this family restaurant serves hearty pancake breakfasts and simple meals throughout the day.

Soft Rock Internet Cafe
$
633 Connaught Dr.
☎*(780) 852-5850*
The Soft Rock Internet Cafe is much more than simply a place to send a few E-mails. It serves up enormous breakfasts all day long.

Spooner's Coffee Bar
$
every day
610 Patricia St.
☎ *(780) 852-4046*
Light meals and freshly squeezed juices are served at Spooner's Coffee Bar. The café has a good selection of tea. The view over the nearby mountains and the young atmosphere combine to make this a very pleasant spot.

The Jasper Marketplace
$-$$
627 Patricia St.
☎ *(780) 852-9676*
The Jasper Marketplace is a pleasant place to have a snack any time of day. Healthy, quality food.

Cantonese Restaurant
$$
every day
across from the bus terminal on Connaught Dr.
☎ *(780) 852-3559*
Cantonese Restaurant serves Szechwan and Cantonese dishes in a typically Chinese decor.

Jasper Pizza Place
$$
402 Connaught Drive
☎ *(780) 852-3225*
Jasper Pizza Place serves up a good selection of pizzas cooked in a conventional oven. Many original combinations are offered: spinach and feta cheese, Mexican with jalapeños…

L&W Restaurant
$$
corner Hazel Ave. and Patricia St.
☎ *(780) 852-4441*
The L&W Restaurant is a family-style restaurant that serves steaks, spaghetti and other dishes in a beautiful dining room filled with plants.

Denjiro
$$
410 Connaught Dr.
☎ *(780) 852-3780*
Denjiro serves tasty Japanese food. The sukiyaki is excellent, but the gloomy decor is not.

Outside Jasper

Becker's Chalets
$75-$150 per cabin
&, tv, K, ℜ
on Icefields Parkway
5 km south of Jasper
Box 579, Jasper, AB, T0E 1E0
☎ *(780) 852-3779*
≈ *(780) 852-7202*
Becker's Chalets, also located along the Athabasca River, are comfortable and well-equipped. A laundromat is on the premises. The restaurant (*$$*) serves fine traditional dishes, though in a rather impersonal decor.

Pine Bungalow Cabins
$75-$100
&, K
on Hwy. 16
near the Jasper golf course
Box 7, Jasper, AB, T0E 1E0
☎ (780) 852-3491
≈ (780) 852-3432

Pine Bungalow Cabins fit the category of a motel. The cabins are fully equipped, with some even have fireplaces. The furnishings, however, are very modest and in rather poor taste. All the same, it is one of Jasper's cheapest places to stay.

Jasper House
$80-$168
tv, K, ℜ
a few kilometres south of Jasper
on Icefields Parkway
at the foot of Mount Whistler
Box 817, Jasper AB T0E 1E0
☎ (780) 852-4535
≈ (780) 852-5335

Jasper House consists of a group of little chalet-style log houses built along the Athabasca River. Comfortable and quiet, the rooms are big and well equipped.

Pyramid Lake Resort
$89-$189
summer only
&, tv, ℜ
on the shore of Pyramid Lake
5km from Jasper
take Pyramid Lake Rd.
to Jasper and follow the signs
to Lake Patricia and Pyramid Lake
Box 388, Jasper, AB, T0E 1E0
☎ (780) 852-4900
☎ (780) 852-3536
≈ (780) 852-7007

Pyramid Lake Resort offers simple but comfortable rooms facing Pyramid Lake where you can enjoy your favourite nautical activities. Rentals of motorboats, canoes, and water-skis are available at the hotel. The restaurant (*$*) serves up simple, well-made meals.

Alpine Village
$100-$200 per cabin
tv, K, ℝ, ⊛
2km south of Jasper
near the cutoff for Mount Whistler
Box 610, Jasper, AB T0E 1E0
☎ (403) 852-3285

Alpine Village is an attractive group of comfortable little wood cabins. Facing the Athabasca River, the spot is calm and peaceful. If possible, ask for one of the cabins facing the river directly: these are the most pleasant. Reserve far in advance, as early as January for the summer. The restaurant (*$$*) here does not have a particulary pleasant decor

Jasper 43

The Rocky Mountains

Miette Hot Springs

Miette Hot Spring Bungalows
$5-$80
K, ℜ
next to the Miette Hot Springs
Jasper East, Box 907, Jasper, AB,
T0E 1E0
☎*(780) 866-3750*
☎*(780) 866-3760, in the off-season*
☎*(780) 852-4039*
≠*(780) 866-2214*
Miette Hot Spring Bungalows offers accommodations in bungalows and a motel. Though the motel rooms are rather ordinary, those in the bungalows offer good quality.

Pocahontas Bungalows
$75-$110 per cabin
✻, K
on Hwy. 16, near Punchbowl Falls
Box 820, Jasper, AB, T0E 1E0
☎*(780) 866-3732*
☎*800-843-3372*
≠*(780) 866-3777*
Pocahontas Bungalows is a small group of cabins located at the entrance to Jasper National Park on the road leading to Miette Hot Springs. The least expensive cabins do not have kitchenettes.

Hinton and Surroundings

Suite Dreams B&B
$75-$100 bkfst incl
tv, ≡
When you arrive at the junction with the 40N, turn right toward the south, then immediately left onto William's Road.
☎*(780) 865-8855 or 865-4381*
Located a few kilometres before Hinton, Suite Dreams B&B is a superb Victorian-style home that has three magnificently decorated bedrooms. Reserve early during the summer season.

Black Cat Guest Ranch
$82 per person, fb
pb, ⊛
Box 6267, T7V 1X6
☎*(780) 865-3084*
☎*800-859-6840*
≠*(780) 865-1924*
www.telusplanet.net/public/bcranch/
The Black Cat provides a peaceful retreat and lots of family fun that is, ideal for family get-togethers. There are guided trail rides, hiking trails and cross-country skiing in the winter. The accommodations are rustic and homey and each room has a mountain view. The scenery can also be enjoyed from the outdoor hot-tub. The ranch also offers theme weekends and organizes excursions. Special rates for children.

Overlander Mountain Lodge
$100-$150
ℜ

2 km to the left after leaving Jasper National Park toward Hinton
Box 6118, Hinton, AB, T7V 1X5
☎ *(780) 866-2330*
≠ *(780) 866-2332*

The Overlander Mountain Lodge has several charming cabins. This establishment is rendered more pleasant by the fact that it is set in a much calmer area than the outskirts of Jasper. The surrounding scenery is truly exquisite. This place stands out from the majority of motel-style establishments in this town. Reservations should be made far in advance, as Hinton is a common alternative to lodging in Jasper. The attractive restaurant *($$$)* here serves excellent food. The menu changes daily. If you have the opportunity, however, give in to temptation and savour the rainbow trout stuffed with crab and shrimp and covered with *béarnaise* sauce.

Athens Corner Restaurant
$
every day
in the Hill Shopping Centre
☎ *(780) 865-3956*

Athens Corner Restaurant offers tried-and-true Canadian dishes as well as Greek and Italian items, all at reasonable prices.

Greentree Café
$
every day 5:30am to 11pm
in the Greentree Motor Lodge
☎ *(780) 865-3321*

Greentree Café prepares delicious, copious breakfasts at unbeatable prices.

Pizza Hut
$
every day
Carmichael Lane
☎ *(780) 865-8455*

The Pizza Hut chain is well known. The variety of pizzas is extensive and reasonably priced.

Ranchers
$
every day
in the Hill Shopping Centre
☎ *(780) 865-4116*

Ranchers prepares all sorts of pizzas. This spot is generally quite busy.

Fireside Dining Room
$$
every day
in the Greentree Motor Lodge
☎ *(780) 865-3321*

Fireside Dining Room is the best and most attractive restaurant in Hinton.

Kootenay National Park

🛏️ 🍴 Kootenay Park Lodge
$74-$92 per cabin
mid-May to late Sep
🐾, ℜ, ℝ
on Hwy 93 heading south
42 km from Castle Junction
Box 1390, Banff, AB, T0L 0C0
☎ *(403) 762-9196*
in the off-season, phone Calgary
☎/≠ *(403)283-7482*

Kootenay Park Lodge rents 10 small log cabins clinging to the steep slopes of the mountains of Kootenay National Park. On site you will find a small store offering sandwiches and everyday items. The restaurant (*$*) is open only from 8am to 10am, 12 to 2pm and 6pm to 8:30pm and offers light meals in simple surroundings.

🛏️ 🍴 Storm Mountain Lodge
$125 per cabin
ℜ
after Castle Mountain Junction
go toward Radium Hot Springs
at your right from the Continental
Divide between Alberta
and British Columbia
Box 670, Banff, AB, T0L 0C0
☎ *(403) 762-4155*

Storm Mountain Lodge is comprised of 12 small cabins at the eastern entrance of Kootenay National Park. The level of comfort is basic, but the setting is enchanting. The small restaurant (*$$*) closes very early, but if you get there on time try the excellent braised salmon or clams. The lodge underwent renovations, reopening in mid-1998.

Radium Hot Springs

Surprisingly accommodations in Radium Hot Springs consist essentially of very ordinary motel rooms. All along the town's main drag, you will find motel fronts that rival each other in ugliness. The region is popular with visitors, however, so here are a few suggestions.

🛏️ Misty River Lodge
$55-$75
🐾, ≡, *tv*, K
5036 Hwy 93, Box 363
Radium Hot Springs, BC, V0A 1M0
☎ *(250) 347-9912*
≠ *347-9397*

Misty River Lodge is the only exception to the "ugly-motel" rule in Radium Hot Springs. The rooms offer a decent level of comfort. The bathrooms are spacious and very clean. Without a doubt, the best motel in town.

🛏️ Both the **Crystal Springs Motel** (*$48-$60*; ♿, *tv*, ⊛; *Box 218, Radium Hot Springs, BC, V0A 1M0*, ☎ *250-347-9759 or 800-347-9759*, ≠ *250-347-9736*) and the **Crescent**

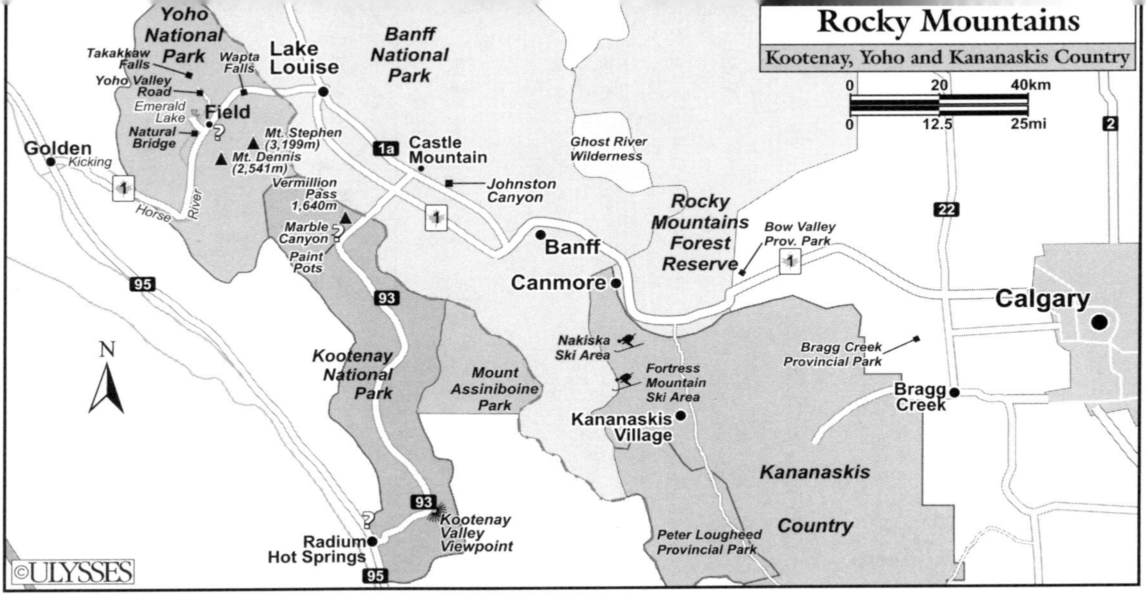
Rocky Mountains
Kootenay, Yoho and Kananaskis Country
0
20
40km
0
12.5
25mi
Yoho National Park
Takakkaw Falls
Yoho Valley Road
Emerald Lake
Field
Natural Bridge
Wapta Falls
Lake Louise
Banff National Park
Golden
Kicking
Horse
River
Mt. Stephen (3,199m)
Mt. Dennis (2,541m)
Castle Mountain
Johnston Canyon
Vermillion Pass 1,640m
Marble Canyon
Paint Pots
Ghost River Wilderness
Rocky Mountains Forest Reserve
Bow Valley Prov. Park
Banff
Canmore
Calgary
Kootenay National Park
Mount Assiniboine Park
Nakiska Ski Area
Fortress Mountain Ski Area
Kananaskis Village
Bragg Creek Provincial Park
Bragg Creek
Kananaskis Country
Peter Lougheed Provincial Park
Kootenay Valley Viewpoint
Radium Hot Springs
N
1a
1
2
22
93
95
©ULYSSES

Motel *($75; tv; Box 116, Radium Hot Springs, BC, V0A 1M0, ☎ 250-347-9570)* have typical motel-style rooms, although the Crescent is definitely not the friendliest place in town.

🛏 Motel Tyrol
$60-$70
△, ≈, ⊛
Box 312, Radium Hot Springs BC, V0A 1M0
☎*(250) 347-9402*

Motel Tyrol offers adequate, modestly furnished rooms and a pleasant terrace by the pool.

🛏 The Chalet
$95
&, ☉, △, tv, ⊛
Box 456, Radium Hot Springs BC, V0A 1M0
☎*(250) 347-9305*
≠*(250) 347-9306*

The Chalet offers several rooms with modestly furnished but comfortable balconies. Perched above the little town of Radium Hot Springs, this large Savoy chalet-style house offers an interesting view of the valley below.

🛏 ✕ Radium Hot Springs Lodge
$100-$125
tv, ℜ, ≈, △
facing the Radium Hot Springs thermal pool
Box 70, Radium Hot Springs, BC, V0A 1M0,
☎*(250) 347-9341*
☎*888-222-9341*
≠*(250) 347-9342*

Radium Hot Springs Lodge has large, extremely ordinary, though modestly furnished, rooms. It's restaurant (*$$*) tries to be chic but serves over-priced food of average quality. All the same, the hotel does have the advantage of being well located and can be considered among the few good spots in Radium Hot Springs.

Fairmont Hot Springs

🎿 🛏 ✕ Fairmont Hot Springs Resort
$139
&, ≈, ℜ, tv, ℝ, ⊛, △, ℜ
on Hwy. 93-95
near the Fairmont ski hills
Box 10, Fairmont Hot Springs BC, V0B 1L0
☎*(250) 345-6311*
☎*800-663-4979*
≠*(250) 345-6616*

Fairmont Hot Springs Resort is a magnificent hotel complex that is wonderfully laid out, offering special spa, ski and golf packages. Hotel guests can also take advantage of tennis courts and two superb 18-hole golf courses. Guests have unlimited access to the hot springs. The restaurant *($$)* at the resort will satisfy the most demanding customers. Its healthy food is excellent, while the decor is pleasant.

Invermere

Delphine Lodge
$60-$80 bkfst incl.
pb/sb, ✖
Main St., Wilmer, V0A 1K0
☎ *(250) 342-6851*

The Delphine Lodge is actually in Wilmer, five kilometres (3.1mi) from Invermere. Though the rooms are a bit small, they and the lodge are packed with lovely antiques and rustic furniture. Handmade quilts, pretty garden, a fireplace and various special little touches make this historic inn (1890s) a cozy favourite. Non-smoking. Small pets only (check ahead).

Panorama Resort
$130-175
≈, ℜ, △, ⊛, *K*
18 km west of Invermere
Box 2797, V0A 1T0
☎*(250) 342-6941*
☎*800-663-2929*
≠*(250) 342-3395*

Panorama Resort offers standard, yet quite nice hotel rooms as well as equipped condo-style units which are particularly handy if you are here to ski, downhill or cross-country. Besides skiing they offer tennis, horseback riding and golf. Pleasant family atmosphere.

Yoho National Park

Emerald Lake Lodge
$165-$275
Box 10, Field, V0A 1G0
☎*(250) 343-6321*
☎*800-663-6336*
≠*(250) 343-6724*

Emerald Lake Lodge, in Yoho National Park, was built by Canadian Pacific in the 1890s and today is an exquisite mountain hideaway. The central lodge built of hand-hewn timber is the hub of activity, while guests stay in one of 24 cabins. Each room features a fieldstone fireplace, willow-branch chairs, a down duvet, a private balcony and terrific lake views. Just 40km (24.9mi) from Lake Louise. The dining room *($$$$)* here is one of the finest in the Canadian Rockies. They serve Rocky Mountain Cuisine, a blend of the fine meals once served in CPR dining cars, the hearty fare once enjoyed by mountain guides and local ingredients like berries and wild game.

Golden and Surroundings

🛏 Columbia Valley Lodge
$55-$75 bkfst incl.
on Hwy 95 a few kilometres south of Golden, Box 2669A
Golden, BC, V0A 1H0
☎/≠ *(250) 348-2508*
Columbia Valley Lodge has 12 rustic rooms. It resembles a mountain refuge with a basic level of comfort, but it is nonetheless completely adequate. This is a good stopping point for cyclists travelling around the area.

🛏 McLaren Lodge
$75 bkfst incl.
above Hwy 95 leaving Golden toward Yoho National Park
Box 2586, Golden, BC
V0A 1H0
☎ *(250) 344-6133*
≠ *(250) 344-7650*
McLaren Lodge is an interesting spot in Golden for nature-lovers. The owners of this little hotel organize river rafting excursions. Rooms are rather small and have a pleasant old-fashioned air. This spot has the best quality-to-price ratio in Golden.

🛏 ✕ Prestige Inn
$110
✖, ♿, K, ⊛, tv, ≈, ℜ, ☺
1049 Trans-Canada Hwy
Box 9, Golden, BC, V0A 1H0
☎ *(250) 344-7990*
≠ *(250) 344-7902*
Prestige Inn is Golden's best hotel. Rooms are quite spacious, and bathrooms are well equipped. The restaurant *($$)* here encompasses the best of traditional cuisine in Golden.

Kananaskis Country

🛏 ✕ Best Western Kananaskis Inn
$160-$180
♿, tv, K, △, ⊛, ≈, ℜ
on the central square of Kananaskis Village, T0L 2H0
☎ *(403) 591-7500*
☎ *800-528-1234*
≠ *(403) 591-7633*
Kananaskis Inn Best Western has 95 comfortable, pleasantly furnished rooms. The atmosphere at this hotel is quite agreeable, and the staff are friendly. However, the lobby is often besieged by visitors searching for souvenir shops or tea rooms.

With its simple but warm decor, the restaurant *($$)* at the inn, has an interesting menu with quite good food.

Lodge at Kananaskis & The Kananaskis Hotel
$285
✘, tv, ℜ, ≈, ◊, ®, ☺
on the central square
of Kananaskis Village, T0L 2H0
☎(403) 591-7711
☎800-441-1414
≠(403) 591-7770

The Lodge at Kananaskis & The Kananaskis Hotel, along with the Hotel Kananaskis, are part of the Canadian Pacific hotel chain. The lodge has 250 spacious, intimate rooms of great comfort. Advance reservations are recommended year-round. The hotel itself offers 70 comfortable rooms and is very pleasant thanks to the friendly staff. **L'Escapade** (*$$$*) is the hotel's French restaurant. Prettily decorated with red carpeting, comfortable armchairs and bay windows, this spot exudes warmth, all the better to linger over the excellent cuisine.

Chief Chiniki
$
every day
on Hwy 21, at Morley
☎(403) 881-3748

Chief Chiniki offers typical North American dishes at reasonable prices. The staff is very friendly and attentive.

Obsessions
$
every day
in Kananaskis Village

Obsessions, a little bar reserved for non-smokers, serves light meals.

Mount Engadine Lodge
$$
Spray Lakes Rd.
☎(403) 678-2880

Mount Engadine Lodge offers an interesting table d'hôte. The European-style cuisine is delicious.

Public Sculpture in Calgary

Calgary

Despite many perceptions to the contrary, a visit to Calgary will likely result in more sightings of people dressed in power suits than Wranglers and Stetsons.

A city of contrasts, it bears the moniker "Cowtown" and is home to the world-famous Calgary Stampede. A thriving economy and a growing urban workforce, however, have brought the former cattle-ranching hub a more cosmopolitan flavour. While the city's pioneer heritage has not been forgotten, the boom-or-bust oil industry has dotted Calgary's skyline with towering office buildings, and the horse-drawn wagons of old have been replaced by bustling highway commuters.

The population of around 800,000 is steadily growing. Migrants from across Canada and around the world are attracted by Calgary's economic prosperity as well as by its enviable proximity to the majestic Rocky Mountains. It is without a doubt a city of business, a metropolis cradled between plains and mountains in the valley where the Bow and Elbow rivers converge.

Accommodations

A large number of quality hotels are available for visitors, many of them conveniently located in the downtown core. Accommodation alternatives do not, however, end outside the city centre. From the airport to the farthest corners of Calgary there are a number of lodging choices available. Prices are generally reasonable, but large hotel chains greatly outnumber the smaller inns and bed and breakfasts. Calgary's Motel Village is an interesting centre of tourism activity. Located just off the Trans-Canada Highway (which runs through the city), and with excellent access to the local transit system, the "village" is home to dozens of hotels.

During the Stampede (early July), Calgary comes alive with the tens of thousands of visitors who arrive to take part in the festivities. As a result, hotels offer a Stampede rate and a rate for the rest of the year. Reservations should be made in advance for those visiting during this time.

There are often two rates for Calgary hotels and motels; a Stampede rate and a rest-of-the-year rate, and the difference between the two can be substantial in some cases.

Bed and Breakfast Association
☎ 543-3900
≠ 543-3901
The Bed and Breakfast Association of Calgary can help you choose among the city's 40 bed and breakfasts.

Restaurants

From fine dining to eating out on a budget, Calgary's restaurants fill every niche. While the city is not as culturally diverse as Vancouver, Toronto or Montréal, there are nevertheless many international dining opportunities. Befitting a former centre of cattle-ranching, the city's steakhouses are excellent, with world-famous Alberta beef having a prominent place on menus. Alberta beef is still, of course, one of the city's specialties. However, the availability of fine seafood and the contribution of the city's varied ethnic communities make for an interesting mix of flavours.

In fact, there is much more to dining in Calgary than a pancake breakfast from the back of a chuckwagon or a juicy steak supper. The city has more than its share of trendy eateries, many of which have the decor down pat and the delicious cuisine to match. The highest

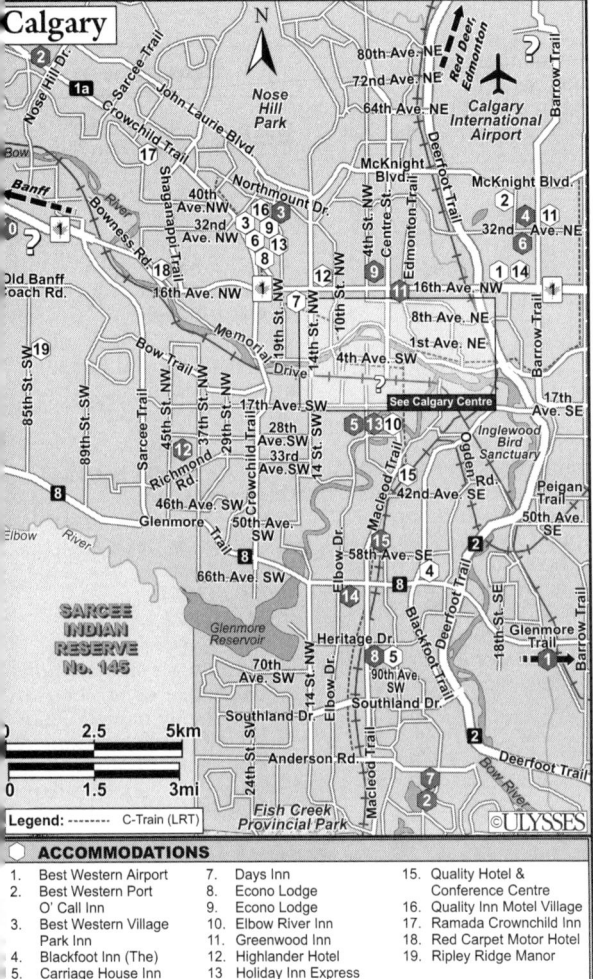

Calgary

ACCOMMODATIONS

1. Best Western Airport
2. Best Western Port O' Call Inn
3. Best Western Village Park Inn
4. Blackfoot Inn (The)
5. Carriage House Inn
6. Comfort Inn
7. Days Inn
8. Econo Lodge
9. Econo Lodge
10. Elbow River Inn
11. Greenwood Inn
12. Highlander Hotel
13. Holiday Inn Express
14. Pointe Inn
15. Quality Hotel & Conference Centre
16. Quality Inn Motel Village
17. Ramada Crownchild Inn
18. Red Carpet Motor Hotel
19. Ripley Ridge Manor

RESTAURANTS

1. Big Rock Grill
2. Brewster Brewing Company and Restaurant
3. Blue House Cafe
4. Carver's Steakhouse
5. Earl's Tin Palace
6. Husky House
7. Inn on Lake Bonavista
8. Joey's Only
9. Mamma's Ristorante
10. Naturbahn Teahouse
11. Peter's Drive-In
12. Primal Grounds
13. Rajdoot
14. Smuggler's Inn
15. Taj Mahal

© ULYSSES

Legend: -------- C-Train (LRT)

concentration of such establishments is in the Southwest in two of Calgary's trendiest neighbourhoods: on or around hip 17th Avenue SW and Fourth Street SW. A dinner-time stroll in these areas will not disappoint the hungry. The only difficulty is choosing between the wide range of great food served in charming settings. After sundown, these neighbourhoods really come alive.

Downtown is no longer the restaurant wasteland that it once was; it now has several good spots along Stephen Avenue and several fine hotel dining rooms. A few gems are also tucked away in the strangest places, like bland strip malls and non-descript semi-basements, so you have to know where to look. Chinatown, nestled between the city centre's skyscrapers, has some fantastic Asian cuisine.

Finally, restaurant prices are very reasonable, so there really is something for everyone.

Blue Jay

Downtown

The Lord Nelson Inn
$95
ℜ, ≡, ⊛, tv, ℝ, K
1020 8th Ave. SW
Calgary, T2P 1J2
☎ *(403) 269-8262*
☎ *800-661-6017*
⇌ *(403) 269-4868*

The Lord Nelson Inn offers reasonably priced hotel accommodation close to downtown and the C-Train.

Quality Hotel and Conference Centre
$99
K, ≈, ⊛, ℜ, ≡
3828 Macleod Tr. S
☎ *(403) 243-5531*
☎ *800-361-3422*
⇌ *(403) 243-6962*

For quality accommodations at reasonable rates, choose the aptly named Quality Hotel and Conference Centre which is very popular with businesspeople. The hotel was renovated in July 1998; its 130 rooms are decorated in a contemporary style with some having kitchenettes. Services include laundry and childcare and there is a restaurant (*$*) on the premises.

Sandman Hotel
$112
ℜ, P, ≡, ≈, ⊛, tv, ☺, △, K
888 7th Ave. SW,
Calgary, T2P 3J3
☎ *(403) 237-8626*
☎ *800-726-3626*
≠ *(403) 290-1238*

Travellers in search of a hotel with facilities and quality rooms should check out the Sandman Hotel. The heated parking and 24hr food services can come in handy.

The Best Western Suites Calgary Centre
$135
ℜ, ≡, tv, K, ☺, △, 🐾
1330 8th St. SW
Calgary, T2R 1B6
☎ *(403) 228-6900*
☎ *800-981-2555*
≠ *(403) 228-5535*

The Best Western Suites Calgary Centre is perhaps one of the best values near the downtown area. All the rooms are suites with one or two bedrooms and kitchenettes.

Prince Royal Inn
$135
ℜ, △, ☺, tv, K
618 5th Ave. SW
Calgary, T2P 0M7
☎ *(403) 263-0520*
☎ *800-661-1592*
≠ *(403) 298-4888*

The weekly, corporate and group rates of the all-suite Prince Royal Inn make this one of the least expensive hotel accommodations right downtown. The fully-equipped kitchens also help keep costs down.

Holiday Inn Calgary Downtown
$179
≈, ⊛, △, ctv
119 12th Ave. SW
☎ *(403) 266-4611*
☎ *800-661-9378*
≠ *(403) 237-0978*

If a great reputation is a must for you, the Holiday Inn Calgary Downtown does not disappoint. Its 180 rooms are especially comfortable. Guests can plug their laptop computers into the outlets provided, rent films directly from the televisions *($7)*, and won't miss any important calls since every telephone has voice mail. The hotel also offers many facilities, including indoor and outdoor pools, a sauna and a whirlpool.

Ramada Crownchild Inn
$135 bkfst incl.
≡, ctv, P, ≈, ☺, ⊛
5353 Crownchild Tr. NW
☎ *(403) 288-5353*
≠ *(403) 286-8966*
www.crownchildinn.com

For lodgings with all the comforts, don't hesitate; reserve a room at the Ramada Crownchild Inn. Set in the centre of Calgary's business district near many good restaurants and just steps from all of the professional sports venues, this hotel has won several prizes including the Good Housekeeping Award. Guests can choose from 60 rooms (rates vary depending on whether the rooms are furnished with double, queen-, or king-size beds), some of which are reserved for non-smokers. Each room has a coffee maker, and a local newspaper is delivered every morning, compliments of the management.

🛏 Calgary Mariott Hotel
$159
ℜ, ≈, ≡, ⊛, △, ⊘, tv, ✗, ♿
110 9th Ave. SE
Calgary, T2G 5A6
☎ *(403) 266-7331*
☎ *800-228-9290*
≠ *(403) 262-8442*

Across the street is the business-class Calgary Mariott Hotel, the biggest of the downtown hotels. Its spacious rooms are decorated with warm colours and comfortable furnishings.

🛏 Sheraton Suites Calgary Eau Claire
$189
P, ≈, ⊛, △, K
255 Barclay Parade SW
☎ *(403) 266-7200*
☎ *888-784-8370*
≠ *(403) 266-1300*

Set in the heart of downtown, the Sheraton Suites Calgary Eau Claire offers more than 300 plush rooms in its 15 storeys. It's the perfect hotel for true luxury-seekers. Among other benefits, the rooms are very spacious with living areas separated from bedrooms by double doors, and all of them have kitchenettes. Guests can take advantage of the hotel's privileged location by shopping at the Eau Claire Market or seeing a film at the IMAX theatre.

○ **ACCOMMODATIONS**	
1. Delta Bow	4. Sheraton Suite Calgary Eau Claire
2. Inglewood B&B	
3. Prince Royal Inn	

● **RESTAURANTS**	
1. Barrely Mill	11. Hy's
2. Buchanan's	12. Joey Tomato's
3. Caesar's Steakhouse	13. La Brezza Ristorante
4. Cajun Charlie's	14. La caille on the Bow
5. Deane House Restaurant	15. Outwest
6. Drinkwater's Grill	16. Owl's Nest
7. Ed's Resstaurant	17. River Cafe
8. Embarcadero Wine and Oyster Bar	18. Sam's Original Restaurant and Bar
9. Good Earth Cafe	19. Silver Dragon
10. Grand Isle	20. Teatro

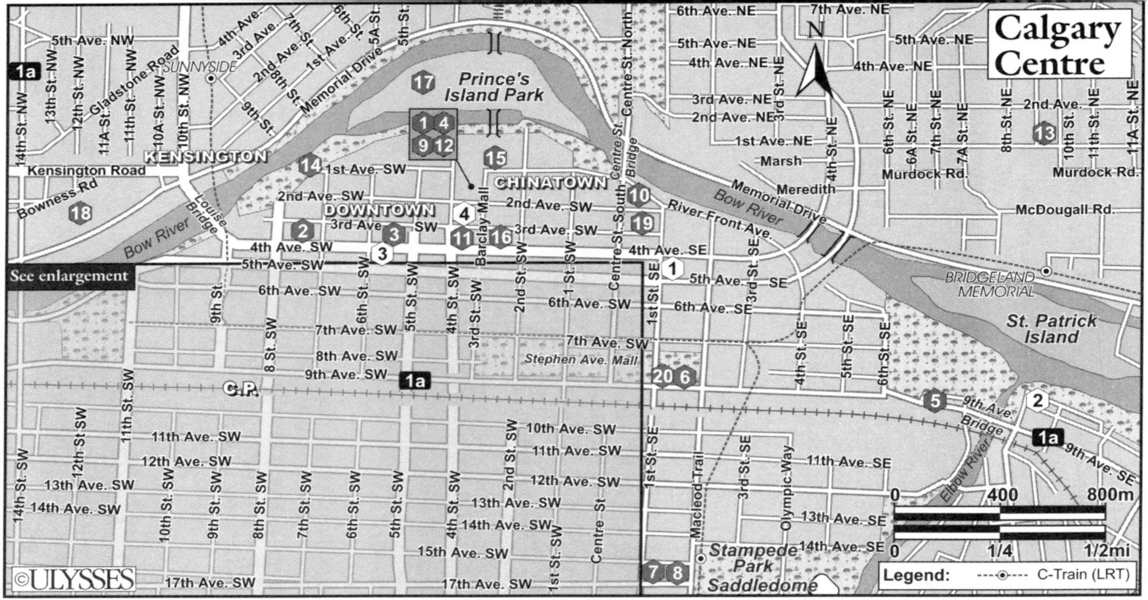

Calgary Centre
Prince's Island Park
KENSINGTON
DOWNTOWN
CHINATOWN
SUNNYSIDE
BRIDGELAND MEMORIAL
St. Patrick Island
Stampede Park
Saddledome
Bow River
Elbow River
Memorial Drive
River Front Ave.
Kensington Road
Bowness Rd
Gladstone Road
Louise Bridge
Centre St. Bridge
9th Ave. Bridge
Barclay Mall
Stephen Ave. Mall
Macleod Trail
Olympic Way
Murdock Rd.
McDougall Rd.
Marsh
Meredith
C.P.
See enlargement
0 400 800m
0 1/4 1/2mi
Legend: C-Train (LRT)
©ULYSSES

🛏 Delta Bow Valley
$260
209 Fourth Ave. SE
☎ *(403) 266-1980*
= *(403) 266-0007*

The Delta Bow Valley is perfectly situated in the heart of Calgary near all the hippest restaurants and cafes. From the top of its 24 storeys, it offers a spectacular view of the city and its surroundings. You should have no trouble getting a room here, since the hotel has 400 in all. Nonetheless, we recommend reservations. If hunger pangs hit, the hotel offers one very chic dining room, The Conservatory, and the more relaxed Coffee Emporium.

🛏 The Palliser
$295-$375
ℜ, ≡, ⊛, △, ⊘, tv, 🐕, ♿
133 9th Ave. SW
Calgary, T2P 2M3
☎ *(403) 262-1234*
☎ *800-441-1414*
= *(403) 260-1260*

The Palliser offers distinguished, classic accommodations in true Canadian Pacific style. The hotel was built in 1914. Restored in 1997, the lofty lobby retains its original marble staircase, solid-brass doors and superb chandelier. The rooms are a bit small but have high ceilings and are magnificently decorated in classic styles.

✕ Break the Fast Cafe
$
516 9th Ave. SW
☎ *(403) 265-5071*

The Break the Fast Cafe is the place to sit back with the newspaper and dig into a hearty breakfast like bacon and eggs, waffles and fresh fruit, custom-made omelettes or a half-kilo of corned-beef hash. Many of the dishes have a Ukrainian twist. The staff can get a bit ragged on busy weekend mornings.

✕ Cedar's Deli
$
225 8th Ave. SW
☎ *(403) 263-0285*
Eau Claire Market
☎ *(403) 263-5232*

Cedar's Deli is a Calgary institution, serving healthy and oh-so-tasty and marvellously spicy Middle-Eastern and Lebanese dishes. It has an almost fast-food ambiance, but offers some of the freshest and tastiest fast food around.

✕ Piq Niq Cafe
$
811 1st St. SW
☎ *(403) 263-1650*

Piq Niq Cafe is an all-day and all-night European cafe with big breakfasts, the ubiquitous panini for lunch and make-your-own-pasta for dinner. It's especially popular for breakfast. There is live jazz on Thursday evenings in the Beat Niq

Jazz and Social Club. As the name suggests, you can even get picnic baskets to go here.

✗ Schwartzie's Bagel Noshery
$
8th Ave. SW
☎ *(403) 296-1353*
If you don't think you'll last until dinner, grab a bagel to go from Schwartzie's Bagel Noshery. Imagine the most typical (sesame or poppy seed) or the most original bagels (chocolate chip, cheese or cinnamon) you can – and they probably have it. You can also eat in; the interior is inviting and comfortable.

🏝 ✗ Sunterra Market
$
Bankers Hall
☎ *(403) 269-3610*
Sunterra Bistro
$
3rd Floor, 401 9th Ave. SW
☎ *(403) 263-9755*
Sunterra Marketplace
$
Elbow Dr. and 49th Ave. SW
☎ *(403) 287-0554*
All three Sunterra restaurants serve up delicious and hearty cafeteria-style meals to crowds of downtown workers every lunch hour particularly at the first two locations. They are a great place to get a good meal while exploring the city, or even to pick up something to go. Seating can be a problem at the Bankers Hall location.

✗ Divino
$$
closed Sun
817 1st St. SW
☎ *(403) 263-5869*
Divino enjoys an enviable location right downtown in the Grain Exchange Building. Striking mahogany-clad walls, the warm glow of Tiffany-style lamps and smooth jazz make eating here a pleasure. The California-Italian fusion cuisine, prepared with market-fresh ingredients, adds to its appeal. The restaurant does double duty as a cafe and wine bar.

🏝 ✗ Drinkwaters Grill
$$
237 8th Ave. SE
☎ *(403) 264-9494*
Drinkwater's Grill is one of the coolest steakhouses in Calgary; its self-billing as "contemporary" is appropriate. The huge sky-blue columns, modern tableaux, classic dark wooden chairs and upholstered banquettes are appealing. On the menu, there is everything from thin-crust pizza to spinach and strawberry salad, Chilean sea bass and, of course, a range of very acceptable sirloins, strips and other fine cuts, each with original accompaniments. There are theatre specials and a Happy Hour

from 3:30pm to 7pm, Monday to Friday.

✕ The Embassy
$$
516C 9th Ave. SW
☎ (403) 213-3970
The Embassy is a modern, two-level cafe and lounge that serves a fairly hip lunch crowd and keeps the drinks flowing into the wee hours. The menu is limited and tends toward classics featuring original ingredients.

✕ Escoba Cafe and Bar
$$
513 8th Ave. SW
☎ (403) 543-8911
The Escoba Cafe and Bar, in Penny Lane Mall, is a South American cafe with rustic stone-clad walls and robust and saucy comfort food to match. Breakfast is one of the most popular

ACCOMMODATIONS
1. Best Western Suites Calgary Centre
2. Calgary Marriot Hotel
3. Holiday Inn Calgary Downtown
4. Sandman Hotel
5. The Nelson Inn
6. The Palliser

RESTAURANTS
1. 4th Street Rose
2. Break the Fast Cafe
3. Brewster Brewing Company and Restaurant
4. Buon Giorno
5. Buzzard's Cowboys Cuisine
6. Byblos Kitchen
7. Cannery Row/McQueen's Upstairs
8. Cedar's Deli
9. Celadon Café and Lounge
10. Chianti
11. Cilantro
12. Dapaoco Ristorante
13. Delectable Delights
14. Divino
15. Entre Nous
16. Escoba Cafe & Bar
17. Fiore Cantina Italiana
18. Florentine
19. Forbidden Flavors
20. Galaxie Diner
21. Huskey House
22. Indochine
23. Khublai
24. Kremlin
25. La Chaumière
26. Mescalero
27. Mongolie Grill
28. Moti Mahal
29. Nellie's Kitchen
30. Panorama Dining Room
31. Pegasus
32. Piq Niq Cafe
33. Rimrock Room
34. Rose & Crown Club
35. Savoir Fare
36. Schwartzie's Bagel Noshery
37. Sukiyaki House
38. Sultan's Tent
39. Sunterra Bistro
40. Sunterra Market
41. Thai Sa-On
42. The Embassy
43. The King & I Thai Restaurant
44. Victoria's Restaurants
45. Virginia's
46. Virginia's Market Café

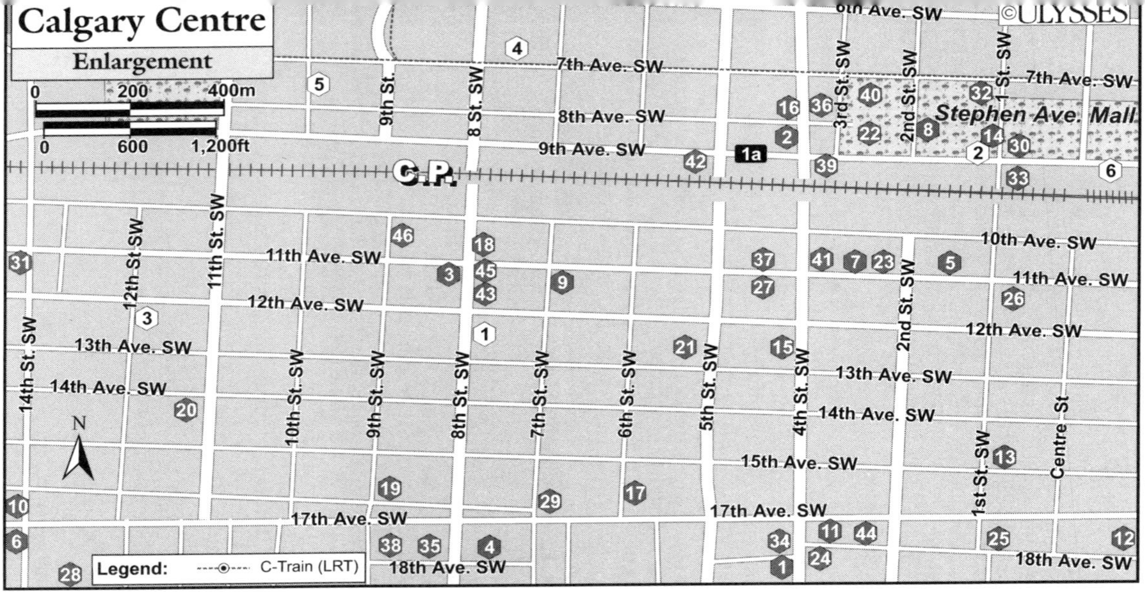
Calgary Centre
Enlargement
0
200
400m
0
600
1,200ft
©ULYSSES
6th Ave. SW
7th Ave. SW
8th Ave. SW
9th Ave. SW
10th Ave. SW
11th Ave. SW
12th Ave. SW
13th Ave. SW
14th Ave. SW
15th Ave. SW
17th Ave. SW
18th Ave. SW
Stephen Ave. Mall
14th St. SW
12th St SW
11th St. SW
10th St. SW
9th St.
9th St. SW
8 St. SW
8th St. SW
7th St. SW
6th St. SW
5th St. SW
4th St. SW
3rd St. SW
2nd St. SW
1 St. SW
1st St. SW
Centre St
C.P.
1a
N
Legend:
C-Train (LRT)

times here with the handful of original homemade waffles A menu of fusion cuisine, martini specials and a good wine selection keeps customers happy the rest of the time.

✗ Indochine
$$
2nd floor Bankers Hall
☎ *(403) 263-6929*

Indochine exudes stark Asian chic with its artfully arranged orchids and even more fabulous plate presentations. The cuisine is a tasty and stylish combination of French and Vietnamese.

✗ Panorama Dining Room
$$-$$$
at the Calgary Tower
Centre St. at 9th Ave. S
☎ *(403) 266-7171*

The Panorama Dining Room is a revolving restaurant with a terrific view of the city by night or by day. The interior decor does not quite live up to the view or the four-course dinner menu and three-course lunch menu. Menus change seasonally. The autumn game menu with regional and international flavours is among the highlights.

✗ Teatro
$$$
200 8th Ave. SE
☎ *(403) 290-1012*

Teatro, right next to Olympic Plaza in the old Dominion Bank Building, boasts a great setting and stylish atmosphere. Traditional "Italian Market Cuisine," prepared in a wood-burning oven, becomes innovative and exciting in the hands of Teatro's chef Dany Lamote.

✗ Caesar's Steakhouse
$$$$
512 4th Ave. SW
☎ *(403) 264-1222*
10816 Macleod Tr. S
☎ *(403) 278-3930*

Caesar's Steakhouse is one of Calgary's most popular spots to dig into a big juicy steak, though they also serve good seafood. The elegant decor features Roman columns and soft lighting.

✗ Hy's
$$$$
316 4th Ave. SW
☎ *(403) 263-2222*

Hy's has been around since 1955 and is the other historic favourite for steaks. The main dishes are just slightly less expensive than Caesar's, and the atmosphere is a bit more relaxed thanks to wood panelling. Reservations are recommended.

Owl's Nest
$$$$
in the Westin Hotel
4th Ave. and 3rd St. SW
☎ *(403) 266-1611*

Fine French and European dishes are artfully prepared at the Owl's Nest. Some are even prepared at your table and flambéed right in front of you. All of the women receive a rose at this fancy dining establishment.

Rimrock Room
$$$$
133 9th Ave. SW
☎ *(403) 262-1234*

The Palliser Hotel's Rimrock Room serves a fantastic Sunday brunch and, of course, healthy portions of prime Alberta beef. The Palliser's classic surroundings and fine food coalesce into one of Calgary's most elegant dining experiences.

Along the Bow River

Ripley Ridge Manor
$95-$125, bkfst incl.
ctv, ℜ
430 85th St. SW
☎ *(403) 288-3415*
☎ *877-344-3400*
≠ *(403) 286-7760*

Overlooking the Bow River and Calgary's outlying area, the Ripley Ridge Manor is a bed and breakfast that offers all the peace of the country less than 15min from downtown. Nature lovers will especially appreciate this establishment because it adjoins a 3.5-hectare (8.6 acres) lot crisscrossed by paths where visitors can stroll and listen to the chattering of birds. Comfort and luxury sum up the atmosphere of this charming inn. Guests can choose from three types of accommodation: suites, "Country Cabins", or the "Guest House". The establishment is also located right next to Canada Olympic Park.

Inglewood Bed & Breakfast
$70
1006 8th Ave. SE
Calgary, T2G 0M1
☎/≠ *(403) 262-6570*

One of the most charming places to stay is Inglewood Bed & Breakfast. Not far from downtown, this lovely Victorian house is also close to the Bow River's pathway system. Breakfast is prepared by Chef Valinda.

Good Earth Cafe
$
at Eau Claire Market
200 Barclay Parade SW
☎ *(403) 237-8684*

The Good Earth Cafe is a wonderful coffee shop with tasty wholesome goodies all made from scratch. Besides being a choice spot for lunch, this is also a good place to go for picnic fixings.

✕ Sam's Original Restaurant and Bar
$-$$
1167 Kensington Cresc. NW
☎ *(403) 270-3880*
Sam's Original Deli and Restaurant is a good spot for lunch while strolling through Kensington. Yummy chicken sandwiches, gourmet burgers, and Montréal-style smoked meat are among the main course offerings, while there are cheesecake, double-fudge cake and to-die-for apple crisp for dessert. The good, solid food far outweighs the mediocre decor as a reason to choose Sam's. Also located at 933 17th Avenue SW and 2208 4th Street SW.

✕ Barley Mill
$$
201 Barclay Parade SW
next to the Eau Claire Market
☎ *(403) 290-1500*
Macleod Tr. S
☎ *(403) 244-6626*
The Barley Mill is located in what appears to be an historic building, but is actually a new construction. An old-fashioned ambiance is successfully achieved with worn-down hardwood floors, a grand fireplace, an old cash register and a bar that comes all the way from Scotland. The menu includes pasta, meat and chicken dishes as well as several imported beers on tap. The newer Macleod Trail location is larger.

✕ Cajun Charlie's
$$
Eau Claire Market
☎ *(403) 233-8101*
Cajun Charlie's is a real hoot in the market, with its Mardi Gras masks, trombone and giant alligator crawling out of the wall. Gumbo and jambalaya are, of course, among the offerings, but so are "voodoo wings" and Po'Boy sandwiches. Blues music adds to the ambience.

✕ Deane House Restaurant
$$
year-round
Wed to Sun 11am to 2pm
806 9th Ave. SE
just across the bridge from Fort Calgary
☎ *(403) 269-7747*
The historic Deane House Restaurant is a pleasant tearoom located in the house of former commanding RCMP officer Richard Burton Deane. Soups and salads figure prominently on the menu.

✕ Grand Isle
$$
128 2nd St. SE
☎ *(403) 269-7783*
Grand Isle prepares many of the favourites of Cantonese cooking but prides itself

on its fresh and light dishes and its Szechuan-inspired flavours. The decor is understated and the staff particularly friendly.

Joey Tomato's
$$
208 Barclay Place SW
next to the Eau Claire Market
☎ *(403) 263-6336*
The open concept at Joey Tomatoes makes for a lively atmosphere. The Italian food includes a great selection of pastas that are topped, by, among other things, original tomato sauces. House wine is by the jug!

Outwest
$$
Eau Claire Market
☎ *(403) 262-9378*
Outwest is a study in the decor of the old west, having been designed by none other than the set creators of the films *Unforgiven* and *Legends of the Fall*. The typical old west cooking has a decidedly original and modern twist; how about venison tortellini to start? Unfortunately, the food does not quite live up to the decor.

Silver Dragon
$$
106 3rd Ave. SE
☎ *(403) 264-5326*
The Silver Dragon is one of the best of the many Chinese restaurants in Chinatown. The staff is very friendly and the dumplings especially tasty.

Stromboli Inn
$$
1147 Kensington Cresc. NW
☎ *(403) 283-1166*
Stromboli Inn offers unpretentious service and ambiance and classic Italian cuisine. Locals recommend it for its pizza, though the menu also includes handmade gnocchi, plump ravioli and a delicious veal gorgonzola.

River Cafe
$$-$$$
Prince's Island Park
☎ *(403) 261-7670*
The River Cafe is now open year-round. You can enjoy regional dishes like wild boar with chanterelle mushrooms and barley risotto or caribou with rosemary and Saskatoon-berry on a crisp fall's day, warm summer's afternoon or frosty winter's eve in beautiful Prince's Island Park. Located in an old boathouse, this gem of a restaurant is the perfect escape from urban downtown Calgary, just across the Bow River. Reservations are highly recommended.

La Brezza Ristorante
$$$
990 1st Ave. NE
☎ *(403) 262-6230*
La Brezza Ristorante serves up inventive Italian pastas with East African spices and

other exotic flavourings. The former private house has been cleverly converted into an intimate restaurant setting. Not far from downtown, this place is popular at lunch and dinner. Reservations are recommended.

Buchanan's
$$$
738 3rd Ave. SW
☎ *(403) 261-4646*

Buchanan's gets the nod not only for its innovative steaks and chops in blue cheese sauce, but also for its excellent wine list (fine choices by the glass) and an impressive selection of single malt scotches. This is a power-lunch favourite with Calgary's business crowd.

La Caille on the Bow
$$$
805 1st Ave. SW
☎ *(403) 262-5554*

La Caille on the Bow occupies a rustic fieldstone building with a distinctly French-Canadian manor feel. Right on the Bow, it is two restaurants in one with formal dining upstairs and casual downstairs. The cuisine is continental and North American.

The South

Elbow River Inn
$89 bkfst incl.
ctv, P
1919 Macleod Tr. SE
☎ *(403) 269-6771*
☎ *800-661-1463*
≠ *(403) 237-5181*

The idyllic setting of the Elbow River Inn will delight even the most discriminating travellers. On the bank of the Elbow River south of Calgary, the hotel offers guests the pleasure of sipping rich coffee on a riverside patio to the sound of birdsong. This establishment meets every requirement, from dining to entertainment, as it houses the restaurant Granny's Kitchen and a casino. For those who would like to make a few purchases, Chinook Centre, a shopping mall of about 200 stores that sell clothing and toys, is just a short walk away.

Saddledome

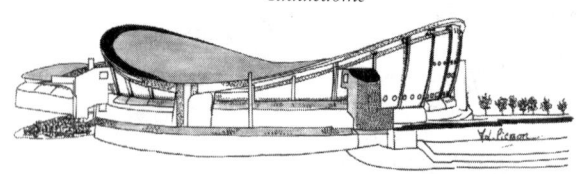

Carriage House Inn
$125
○, P, ⊛, ≈
9030 Macleod Tr. S
☎ *(403) 253-1101*
☎ *800-661-9566*
≠ *(403) 259-2414*

Typical Western Canadian hospitality awaits at the Carriage House Inn which offers 157 rooms with undeniable charm, some of which are reserved for non-smokers. The management has equipped every room with a coffee maker, so guests can brew their own morning coffee and then open the door to find a local daily at their feet. People visiting Calgary on business or travelling with laptop computers will be delighted to find that every room has a modem outlet. The rooms also have minibars. For meals, there are two restaurants; the Bristol Terrace Coffee Shop and the Savoy Dining Lounge.

The Blackfoot Inn
$99
≈, ⊛, ℜ
5940 Blackfoot Tr. SE
☎ *(403) 252-2253*
☎ *800-661-1151*
≠ *(403) 252-3574*
www.blackfootinn.com

Located just a 10min walk from downtown, the Blackfoot Inn has 200 cheerful rooms in which guests can unwind on very cozy beds and plan their vacations at large tables surrounded by comfortable chairs. The outdoor pool and terrace are very popular places to lounge and savour tall, cool beers. If you would rather not head off in search of a restaurant, you can dine at one of the hotel's two eateries: Green's Restaurant and the Terrace Dining Room. The establishment also offers entertainment in the form of Yuk Yuk's Comedy Cabaret and the Other Side Sports Bar. The smiling and attentive staff make a stay here that much more enjoyable.

Byblos Kitchen
$
1449 17th Ave. SW
☎ *(403) 541-1788*

Byblos Kitchen makes a nice change from steak, Italian or fusion. With savoury Mediterranean and Lebanese dishes like falafel, hummus and baba ghanouj.

Chianti
$
17th Ave. SW
☎ *(403) 229-1600*
10816 Macleod Tr. S
☎ *(403) 225-0010*

Chianti on 17th Avenue was recently redone, and is very trendy. This is probably the city's most reasonably priced Italian restaurant. It is known for its pasta, of course, but also for its veal. Reservations recommended. Pasta night on Tuesdays is a particularly good night for budget diners, since any pasta on the menu is $5.75.

✕ Delectable Delights
$

132 15th Ave. SW
☎ *(403) 263-1450*
Delectable Delights, also called D+Ds, is one of Calgary's best delicatessens, with the standard homemade soup, sandwiches and salads, plus a big buffet brunch on Sundays.

✕ Forbidden Flavours
$

1011 17th Ave. SW
☎ *(403) 244-8628*
The ice-cream at gay-owned Forbidden Flavours isn't forbidden at all. In fact, the only problem is trying to choose from the sweet and creamy display: there are supposedly some 500 flavours to choose from.

✕ Galaxie Diner
$

1413 11th St. SW
☎ *(403) 228-0001*
The Galaxie Diner has a French name in honour of the owner's girlfriend and is resplendent with chrome and red vinyl. Breakfast is served all day long. You can also tuck into this joint's version of the western sandwich, called the Calgary sandwich, which comes on multi-grain bread and is garnished with avocado and the like. The burgers are exactly the way they should be and then there are those oh-so heavenly old-fashioned shakes. Save room for the Double Bubble gum with your bill!

✕ Husky House
$

1201 5th St. SW
☎ *(403) 237-7789*
2525 32nd Ave. NE
☎ *(403) 291-1616*
6130 1A St. SW, Chinook Station
☎ *(403) 253-5012*
Husky House is a veritable roadside diner in downtown Calgary that is perfect for that late-night-snack or morning-after pile of pancakes or bacon and eggs. Its unpretentious, anonymous, cheap and nice and greasy!

✕ Nellie's Kitchen
$

Sun to Fri 8am to 3pm
Sat 8am to 4pm
738b 17th Ave. SW
between 7th and 6th St. SW
☎ *(403) 244-4616*
Everything is made from scratch at the informal Nellie's Kitchen, a neat little rendez-vous for people-watching over lunch.

✕ Primal Grounds
$

3003 37th St. SW
☎ *(403) 240-4185*
Primal Grounds is a quick cappuccino bar and eatery with "homestyle" like hearty soups, snacks, sandwiches,

desserts, and fancy coffees too!

✕ Big Rock Grill
$-$$
5555 76th Ave. SE
☎ *(403) 720-3239*

Big Rock Grill, located at the Big Rock Brewery, is a pub-style eatery with all the Big Rock brews on tap, plus grilled dishes on the menu. Don't miss the brewery tour; tours must be reserved ahead of time.

✕ Brewster Brewing Company and Restaurant
$-$$
755 Lake Bonavista Dr. SE
☎ *(403) 255-BREW*
834 11th Ave. SW
☎ *(403) 261-BREW*
151 Crawford Cr. NW
☎ *(403) 208-2739*

Brewster Brewing Company and Restaurant brews 12 premium ales on site and also cooks up the requisite pizzas and snack food to go with it. You can also tour the brewery.

✕ Buon Giorno
$-$$
823 17th Ave. SW
☎ *(403) 244-5522*

Buon Giorno serves authentic northern Italian cooking. Chef Battistessa prepares a special three-course meal for two called l'Abbuffata which is worth the extra effort and money. This classy trattoria has a cozy fireplace.

✕ Celadon Cafe and Lounge
$-$$
720 11th Ave. SW
☎ *(403) 261-2600*

Celadon Cafe and Lounge, in the renovated Building bloc on 11th Avenue SW, has lots of hip new neighbours. Here you can make a meal of the Asian-inspired tapas or fingerfood.

✕ Ed's Restaurant
$-$$
202 17th Ave. SE
☎ *(403) 262-3500*

Ed's Restaurant occupies an old house dating from 1911, with five intimate dining rooms. Credited with bringing the ubiquitous buffalo-style chicken wing to Calgary, Ed also serves traditional dishes stuff like pasta, Alberta beef and seafood.

✕ Pegasus
$-$$
1101 14th St. SW
☎ *(403) 229-1231*

Pegasus has all the classics: moussaka, tsaziki, *keftedes* (spiced meatballs), and good fresh seafood served in an atmospheric crisp white and sea blue decor.

✕ Rose & Crown Pub
$-$$
1503 4th St. SW
☎ *(403) 244-7757*

The Rose & Crown Pub is located in a supposedly haunted old building. Popular with ex-pats and visitors, this authentic English pub serves fish and chips, shepherd's pie and the like, plus more than 30 kinds of beer on tap. It's attractive and cozy, with wing chairs by the fireplace and the warm patina of the all-wood bar.

✘ Taj Mahal
$-$$
4816 Macleod Tr. SW
☎ *(403) 243-6362*
Taj Mahal is located far down on Macleod Trail amidst the car dealers and strip malls. Nonetheless, this basement Indian restaurant serves up delicious authentic tikkas and curries. Comfortable and very friendly.

✘ Virginia's Market Cafe
$-$$
827 10th Ave. SW
☎ *(403) 233-8155*
Virginia's Market Cafe, around the corner from Virginia's Restaurant (see p 76), is like the original Virginia's. However, it has an emphasis on fresh: fresh-cut flowers, freshly brewed coffee, fresh-baked bread and pastries and fresh produce. Known for its gourmet hamburgers.

✘ Buzzard's Cowboy Cuisine
$$
140 10th Ave. SW
☎ *(403) 264-6959*
Buzzard's Cowboy Cuisine conjures up nostalgic chuckwagon-living in the big city. The menu features such items as buffalo chili, whiskey sausage and Buzzard's Breath Ale. Bottlescrew Bill's Pub next door has 150 other brews to choose from.

✘ Da Paolo Ristorante
$$
121 17th Ave. SE
☎ *(403) 228-5556*
Everything you eat here was made on the premises by Paolo de Minico. While this is quite a small place, that's what makes it so good.

✘ Earl's Tin Palace
$$
2401 4th St. SW
☎ *(403) 228-4141*
Earl's Tin Palace is part of the Earl's chain, but is much hipper than most. So much so, in fact, that three of its busboys were recently discovered on the job by modelling scouts from Miami and Milan. The menu is extensive and original with something to please fussy little ones as well as more mature and discerning palates.

✘ Embarcadero Wine and Oyster Bar
$$
208 17th Ave. SW
☎ *(403) 263-0848*
The Embarcadero Wine and Oyster Bar, set in an historic red-brick house, serves up a fine selection of fresh

oysters plus a large menu with everything from pasta and trendy thin-crust pizzas to the house specialty of rack of lamb.

✕ Fiore Cantina Italiana
$$
638 17th Ave. SW
☎ *(403) 244-6603*

The Fiore Cantina Italiana prides itself on freshly-made pastas and a delicious selection of home-made desserts. The daily special is usually the most interesting and tastiest choice.

✕ 4th Street Rose
$$
2116 4th St. SW
☎ *(403) 228-5377*

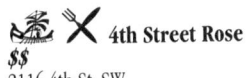

The 4th Street Rose is a favourite. The very Californian fusion cuisine features lots of tasty vegetarian selections like Thai stir-fries and wraps, pasta dishes with wonderfully fresh ingredients and sinfully sweet desserts to finish it all off. On warm summer days, the terrace is the place to be.

✕ Florentine
$$
1014 8th St. SW
☎ *(403) 232-6028*

Florentine is a stylish Italian place with a big-city feel, but its simple, small menu doesn't necessarily offer many choices. Rest assured, however; what's on the menu is fresh and deliciously prepared. The menu changes with the seasons. Save room for dessert.

✕ Joey's Only
$$
811 17th Ave. SW
☎ *(403) 228-4454*

Joey's Only is the family seafood restaurant *extraordinaire*, with unlimited refills for soft drinks and French fries, and all-you-can-eat fish and chips on Tuesday evenings! Casual and fun.

✕ Khublai
$$
349 10th Ave. SW
☎ *(403) 232-8800*

Khublai serves Mongolian cuisine. The experience of eating here is definitely memorable, while the 15 savoury sauces are pretty unique, too. You make your selections from the meat, vegetables and tofu on the raw buffet which is then cooked for you on a giant hooded grill and brought to your table with rice or a wrap. With meals priced by weight, the bill can add up quickly if you aren't careful, though an inexpensive meal is still possible.

✕ The King & I Thai Restaurant
$$
822 11th Ave. SW
☎ *(403) 264-7241*

The King & I Thai Restaurant features an extensive

Calgary

menu of exotic dishes including delicious chu chu kai, Thai curries, banana leaves and chicken wrapped in pandulus. The ambiance is modern and elegant.

✕ Kremlin
$$
2004 4th St. SW
☎(403) 228-6068

The tiny Kremlin serves Russian "love food" that you will fall in love with. Hearty borscht with herb bread is a real deal, or maybe you'll go for the perogies with their filling of the day or the oh-so-tender tenderloin with rosemary, red wine and honey. For dessert, who could say no to perogies filled with Saskatoon-berries and topped with orange brandy cream sauce? The decor is eclectic, cozy and really lives up to the aphrodisiac theme.

✕ Mongolie Grill
$$
1108 4th St. SW
☎(403) 262-7773
5005 Dalhousie Sr. NW
☎(403) 286-7779

The Mongolie Grill, the other Mongolian restaurant in town, is truly a culinary experience. Diners choose meats and vegetables from a fresh food bar. The combination is then weighed (to determine the cost) and grilled right before your eyes. Roll it all up in a Mongolian wrap with some rice and sauce and voilà! This is a big place that is not for those in search of an intimate evening out.

✕ Moti Mahal
$$
507 17th Ave. SW
☎(403) 228-9990

While there are other restaurants of the same name in Canada, this Moti Mahal has a style all its own with its tapestry-covered walls and tasty northern Indian cuisine.

✕ Rajdoot
$$
2424 4th St. SW
☎(403) 245-0181

Rajdoot serves mild northern Indian cuisine along with spicier offerings from the south like Tandoori. Rajdoot was named best Indian restaurant in Calgary in 1996. The lunch buffet and vegetarian buffet are popular. Another big draw is the Sunday brunch.

✕ Victoria's Restaurant
$$
306 17th Ave. SW
☎(403) 244-9991

The decor of Victoria's Restaurant is a tribute to Victorian times and so is the menu, sort of, with chicken pot pie, liver and onions but also pirogies and Asian stir fries, burgers and salads. Sunday brunch.

Cilantro
$$-$$$
338 17th Ave. SW
☎ *(403) 229-1177*
Cilantro puts this seasoning to good use in its original Southwestern cuisine. Weathered wood and iron predominate, and there is a wood-burning pizza oven.

Entre Nous
$$-$$$
2206 4th St. SW
☎ *(403) 228-5525*
Entre Nous, which means "between you and me," is a friendly and intimate bistro that is perfect for savouring some good French food. From the hand-selected ingredients to the table d'hôte menu, special attention to detail make for a memorable dining experience. Reservations recommended.

Savoir Fare
$$-$$$
907 17th Ave. SW
☎ *(403) 245-6040*
Savoir Fare describes itself as a 21st-century diner. This translates, in this case anyway, into a modern, very swish interior and a menu with hifalutin' descriptions and versions of home-cooked favourites like meatloaf. The kitchen also whips up a delicious caramelized dessert. The restaurant is smoke-free and brunch is served on Sundays.

Smuggler's Inn
$$-$$$
6920 Macleod Tr. S
☎ *(403) 253-5355*
Smuggler's Inn, which has been in business for 27 years, offers a juicy selection of quality Alberta steaks including your choice of prime rib running anywhere from six ounces to two pounds. While they also have seafood, chicken, pasta and vegetarian dishes, remember it is the steaks they are known for. Stately high-backed chairs, fireplaces, and antiques set the mood.

Sukiyaki House
$$-$$$
517 10th Ave. SW
☎ *(403) 263-3003*
Sukiyaki House serves traditional Japanese sushi, tempura and teryaki in a traditional Japanese decor with Japanese music, tatami rooms and an indoor garden. The sushi comes highly recommeneded. Good lunch specials.

Thai Sa-On
$$-$$$
351 10th Ave. SW
☎ *(403) 264-3526*
Thai Sa-On gets the nod from locals in the know as the place to go for some of the best Thai cooking in the city. The vegetarian menu is inventive and very tasty. Popular lunch buffet.

Cannery Row
$$$
317 10th Ave. SW
☎ (403) 269-8889
Cannery Row serves this landlocked city's best seafood. An oyster bar and casual atmosphere is intended to make you feel like you're by the sea, and it works. Fresh halibut, salmon and swordfish are prepared in a variety of ways.

McQueen's Upstairs
$$$
317 10th Ave. SW
above Cannery Row
☎ (403) 269-4722
McQueen's Upstairs has a seafood-oriented menu similar to that of the Cannery Row but is slightly more upscale.

Mescalero
$$$
1315 First St. SW
☎ (403) 266-1133
Mescalero serves up an eclectic blend of Southwestern, Mexican and Spanish cuisine, including simply divine veal cheeks that are all cooked on an applewood-fired grill. There is a great courtyard, but unfortunately the service can be mediocre at times.

Sultan's Tent
$$$
909 17th Ave. SW
☎ (403) 244-2333
The Casablancan chef at the Sultan's Tent prepares fine authentic Moroccan cuisine. In keeping with tradition, guests are greeted upon arrival with a basin of scented water with which to wash their hands. The room is decorated with myriad plush cushions and tapestries and the mood is set with lanterns and soft Arabic music. (Remember it is traditional to eat with your right hand.)

Virginia's
$$$
1016 8th St. SW
☎ (403) 294-0890
Virginia's boasts a lofty and spacious interior with solid wooden tables, earthy blue tones and a big river-stone fireplace in the centre of the restaurant; there is even an outdoor terrace! The menu suggests unexpected twists to old favourites, with interesting starters like Tuscan white bean soup or mango-spiced gouda. Then there are the enticing main courses like rabbit roasted in Merlot and herbs, sauteed prawns with Absolut pepper vodka, or slices of fresh peach and butter sauce.

The North

Northeastern Calgary (Near the Airport)

🛏 Pointe Inn
$80
ℜ, ≡, tv, 🐾
1808 19th St. NE
Calgary, T2E 4Y3
☎ *(403) 291-4681*
☎ *800-661-8164*
≠ *(403) 291-4576*

Travellers just passing through or who have early or late flight connections should consider the convenience and reasonable prices of the Pointe Inn. The rooms are clean, but very ordinary. Laundry facilities.

American Robin

🛏 The Best Western Airport
$109
ℜ, ≡, ≈, tv, 🐾
1947 18th Ave. NE
Calgary, T2E 2T8
☎ *(403) 250-5015*
☎ *800-528-1234*
≠ *(403) 250-5019*

The Best Western Airport offers similar accommodations, plus an outdoor pool.

🍴✗ La Chaumiere
$$$$
139 17th Ave. SW
☎ *(403) 228-5590*

La Chaumiere is the French restaurant of choice for special occasions in Calgary. While it looks big from the outside, inside a classy and intimate dining room awaits. The finest china and crystal are laid out and do justice to tasty concoctions such as escargots à l'Abbaye prepared with Pernod, lobster Bisque, magret de canard and veal Calvados. Reservations are recommended and jackets are required for men.

✗ Inn on Lake Bonavista
$$$$
747 Lake Bonavista Dr. SE
☎ *(403) 271-6711*

The Inn on Lake Bonavista is one of Calgary's finest dining rooms with menu selections like filet mignon and Châteaubriand, complemented by lovely views of the lake through floor-to-ceiling picture windows.

🛏 Best Western Port O' Call Inn
$139
ℜ, ≡, ≈, ⊛, tv, ♿
1935 McKnight Blvd. NE
Calgary, T2E 6V4
☎ *(403) 291-4600*
☎ *800-661-1161*
≠ *(403) 250-6827*

Best Western Port O' Call Inn is a full-service hotel with 24-hour shuttle service to the airport that's located close by. Facilities include an indoor pool and a racquetball court.

🛏 Greenwood Inn
$129
ctv, ≡
3515 26th St. NE
☎ *(403) 250-8855*
☎ *888-AFFORD-0*
≠ *(403) 250-8050*

One of the newest hotels in the Calgary region is the Greenwood Inn. Open since March 1998, this 200-room establishment offers travellers several conveniences including coffee makers, hair dryers, voice mail, and, in some rooms, microwave ovens and "sauna-showers." There is also laundry service from Monday to Friday.

✕ Carver's Steakhouse
$$-$$$
at the Sheraton Cavalier
2620 32nd Ave. NE
☎ *(403) 250-6327*

The decor of Carver's Steakhouse was spruced up as part of the Sheraton Cavalier's recent facelift. The modern steakhouse still serves the same triple-A-grade Alberta beef. The service is very attentive. Locals and hotel guests alike appreciate this fine restaurant.

✕ Peter's Drive-In
$
219 16th Ave. NE
☎ *(403) 277-2747*

If you're craving burgers, fries and a shake and it has to be fast, skip the golden arches and head for Calgary's own Peter's Drive-In. With only one location there is always a line-up, but this classic is worth the wait.

Northwestern Calgary (Motel Village)

Calgary's "Motel Village" is quite something: car rental offices, countless chain motels and hotels, fast-food and family-style restaurants and the Banff Trail C-Train stop. The majority of the hotels and motels look the same, but the more expensive ones are usually newer and offer more facilities. Most places charge considerably higher rates during Stampede Week.

Red Carpet Motor Hotel
$49-$89
≡, ℝ, tv, 🐾
4635 16th Ave. NW
Calgary T3B 0M7
☎ *(403) 286-5111*
≠ *(403) 247-9239*

The Red Carpet Motor Hotel is one of the best values in Motel Village. Some suites have small refrigerators.

Highlander Hotel
$59-$149
ℜ, ≡, ≈, tv, 🐾
1818 16th Ave.
Calgary T2M 0L8
☎ *(403) 289-1961*
☎ *800-661-9564*
≠ *(403) 289-3901*

The Scottish decor of the Highlander Hotel is a nice change from the typically drab motel experience. Close to services and a shopping mall. Airport shuttle service available.

Econo Lodge
$89
≡, △, ☉, tv
2440 16th Ave. NW
Calgary T2M 0M5
☎ *(403) 289-2561*
≠ *(403) 282-9713*

The Econo Lodge offers clean, standard motel rooms with queen-size beds. There is no charge for making local telephone calls.

Days Inn
$89
K, △, ⊛, tv, 🐾
2369 Banff Tr. NW
Calgary T2M 4L2
☎ *(403) 289-5571*
☎ *800-325-2525*
≠ *(403) 282-9305*

The Days Inn offers free breakfast and movies. The rooms are pleasantly decorated in soft pastel colours, and the staff is friendly.

Comfort Inn
$110
≡, ≈, △, tv
2363 Banff Tr. NW
Calgary T2M 4L2
☎ *(403) 289-2581*
☎ *800-228-5150*
≠ *(403) 284-3897*

Rates at the Comfort Inn include a continental breakfast. Regular rooms are spacious and comfortable; suites are also available.

Econo Lodge
$110
ℜ, ≡, ≈, K, tv, 🐾
2231 Banff Tr. NW
Calgary T2M 4L2
☎ *(403) 289-1921*
≠ *(403) 282-2149*

The Econo Lodge is a good place for families. Children will enjoy the outdoor pool and playground, while the laundry facilities and large units with kitchenettes are very practical. The Louisiana-style family restaurant serves inexpensive *($)* Cajun and Creole food.

Holiday Inn Express
$95
≡, ≈, ⊛, △, ⊙, *tv*, 🐾
2227 Banff Tr. NW
Calgary T2M 4L2
☎ *(403) 289-6600*
☎ *800-HOLIDAY*
≠ *(403) 289-6767*

The Holiday Inn Express offers quality accommodations at affordable prices. Rooms are furnished with king- and queen-size beds, and a complimentary continental breakfast is served.

Quality Inn Motel Village
$99
ℜ, ≈, ≡, ⊛, △, ⊙, *tv*, 🐾
2359 Banff Tr. NW
Calgary T2M 4L2
☎ *(403) 289-1973*
☎ *800-221-2222 or 800-661-4667*
≠ *(403) 282-1241*

The Quality Inn Motel Village has an attractive lobby and an atrium restaurant and lounge. Both rooms and suites are available. Good value for the price.

Best Western Village Park Inn
$109
ℜ, ≡, ≈, ⊛, *tv*, 🐾, ♿
1804 Crowchild Tr. NW
Calgary T2M 3Y7
☎ *(403) 289-0241*
☎ *800-774-7716 or 800-528-1234*
≠ *(403) 289-4645*

The Best Western Village Park Inn is another member of this well-known chain. Guests enjoy many services, including Budget car-rental offices. Rooms are pleasantly furnished with contemporary colour schemes.

Blue House Cafe
$$
3843 19th St. NW
☎ *(403) 284-9111*

The Blue House Cafe doesn't look like much, but the chef's Argentinian creations, especially the fish and seafood dishes, more than make up for it. Another plus is the flamenco and three-finger guitar performances on some evenings. The mood is fairly casual, but slightly dressier in the evenings.

Naturbahn Teahouse
$$
in the summer:
Mon to Sat lunch and tea
11am to 4pm
year-round:
Sunday brunch
Canada Olympic Park
☎ *(403) 247-5465*

The Naturbahn Teahouse, located at the top of the luge and bobsleigh tracks at Canada Olympic Park, is actually in the former starthouse. *Naturbahn*, which means "natural track", no longer serves up luges; nowadays the menu features a delicious Sunday brunch. Reservations are recommended.

✕ Mamma's Ristorante
$$$
320 16th St. NW
☎ (403) 276-9744
Mamma's Ristorante has been serving Italian cuisine to Calgarians for more than 20 years. The ambiance and menu offerings are equally refined. The latter including homemade pasta, veal and seafood dishes.

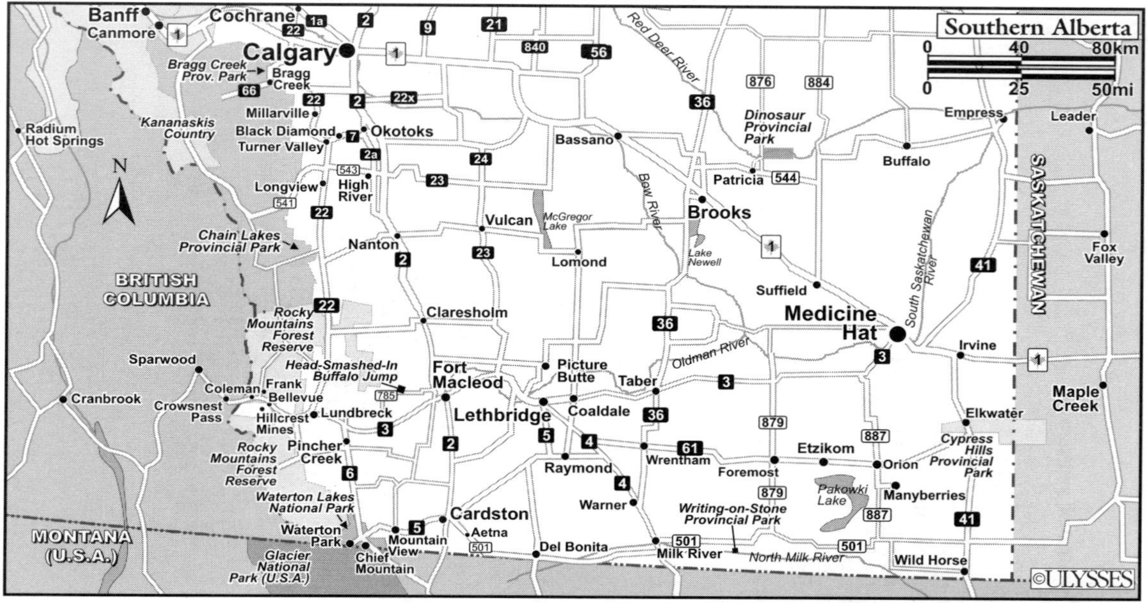
Southern Alberta
0 40 80km
0 25 50mi
Banff
Canmore
Cochrane
Calgary
Bragg Creek Prov. Park
Bragg Creek
Millarville
Black Diamond
Okotoks
Turner Valley
Radium Hot Springs
Kananaskis Country
Longview
High River
Chain Lakes Provincial Park
Nanton
Vulcan
McGregor Lake
Lomond
Bassano
Red Deer River
Bow River
Dinosaur Provincial Park
Patricia
Brooks
Lake Newell
Suffield
Medicine Hat
South Saskatchewan River
Empress
Buffalo
Leader
Fox Valley
SASKATCHEWAN
Irvine
Maple Creek
Elkwater
Cypress Hills Provincial Park
BRITISH COLUMBIA
Rocky Mountains Forest Reserve
Claresholm
Sparwood
Cranbrook
Coleman
Frank
Bellevue
Crowsnest Pass
Hillcrest Mines
Lundbreck
Head-Smashed-In Buffalo Jump
Fort Macleod
Lethbridge
Picture Butte
Coaldale
Taber
Oldman River
Pincher Creek
Waterton Lakes National Park
Waterton Park
Chief Mountain
Mountain View
Cardston
Aetna
Del Bonita
Raymond
Warner
Wrentham
Milk River
Foremost
Etzikom
Orion
Manyberries
Pakowki Lake
Writing-on-Stone Provincial Park
North Milk River
Wild Horse
MONTANA (U.S.A.)
Glacier National Park (U.S.A.)
©ULYSSES

Southern Alberta

On a journey east through southern Alberta, the Rocky Mountains steadily shrink to foothills, then plains, and eventually into conditions that can only be described as desert like.

Hay bales and grain elevators are at times the only noticeable break from an extremely flat terrain with wheat fields as far as the eye can see. Historically, the region developed due to an accident of railway planning. Intending to link Canada from east to west, the Canadian Pacific Railway broke ground in the west in 1881. The route was originally supposed to pass by Edmonton, crossing the Rocky Mountains through Yellowhead Pass. Fearing attack from the United States, however, it was moved to southern Alberta so troops could be sent to Canada's southern border. The cities and towns of the region emerged as a result of the economic opportunities brought by the railway.

The southern arm of the Canadian Rockies passes down through the southwest corner of Alberta. The

Crowsnest Pass area along the border with British Columbia is made up of old coal-mining towns that, while historically interesting, have seen better days. Further east is Waterton Lakes National Park which is an area of stunning natural beauty on the Montana border.

The slow-rolling land east of the Rockies is marked by many small farming communities and two major cities: Lethbridge and Medicine Hat.

Accommodations

Lethbridge – the third-largest city in Alberta after Calgary and Edmonton – is an almost surprising centre of urban activity emerging out of the prairies. Accommodations range from large, comfortable hotel chains to smaller bed and breakfasts. Medicine Hat also offers a number of options.

In the smaller towns stretching from Crowsnest Pass through the southern foothills, camping is a popular choice during the summer. There are still inns and lodges to choose from, many of which feature the charming decor and furnishings of the pioneer era. Those who want to stay in Waterton should keep in mind that many of the town's hotels and motels are closed during the slower winter months.

Restaurants

As is the case throughout the province, fast food joints and mediocre get convenient family-style restaurants are all over southern Alberta. Heavy Western fare can be found throughout the region, but Lethbridge does have a few places that offer some respite from meat and potatoes, including Italian and Asian cuisine. Both Lethbridge and Medicine Hat also have quiet and charming cafés where you can idle a while over a book. With its higher tourist traffic, Waterton has some of the best restaurants and dining rooms in the region.

Crowsnest Pass

The Inn on the Lake
$45 bkfst incl.
sb
$60 cabins
tv, K
2413 23rd Ave.
☎ *(403) 563-5111*
The Inn on the Lake, a lovely country house on Crowsnest Lake, is a cosy

place to enjoy a delicious hot breakfast.

Kosy Knest Kabins
$48
K, tv
Box 670,
Coleman, T0K 0M0
☎/≠(403) 563-5155
You can stay at the Kosy Knest Kabins looking out over Crowsnest Lake, from May 1 to November 1. The 10 cabins are located 12km (7.5mi) west of Coleman on Highway 3.

Waterton

Things slow down considerably during the winter months when many hotels and motels close and others offer winter rates and packages.

The Northland Lodge
$50
sb/pb, ℝ
on Evergreen Ave. Waterton Lakes National Park, T0K 2M0
☎(403) 859-2353
Open from mid-May to mid-October, The Northland Lodge is a converted house with nine cozy rooms. Some rooms have balconies and barbecues.

Black-capped Chickadee

The Kilmorey Lodge
$86
&, ℝ, K
117 Evergreen Ave. Box 100, Waterton Lakes National Park T0K 2M0
☎(403) 859-2334
≠(403) 859-2342
The Kilmorey Lodge is open year-round. Ideally located overlooking Emerald Bay, its many rooms have great views. Antiques and duvets contribute to the old-fashioned, homey feel. Two wheelchair-accessible suites have recently been added. The Kilmorey also boasts one of Waterton's finest restaurants, **The Lamp Post Dining Room**. *($$$)* The traditional charm, coupled with award-winning food and relatively reasonable prices, definitely make it one of the best.

Crandell Mountain Lodge
$116
K, tv, &; 102 Mountview Rd
Box 114
Waterton Lakes National Park, T0K 2M0
☎/≠(403) 859-2288
The small Crandell Mountain Lodge is open from early April until the end of October. Its rustic, homey country-inn atmosphere fits right in with the setting and is a nice change from the motel scene. Four three-room suites with full kitchens are available, and four rooms have kitchenettes.

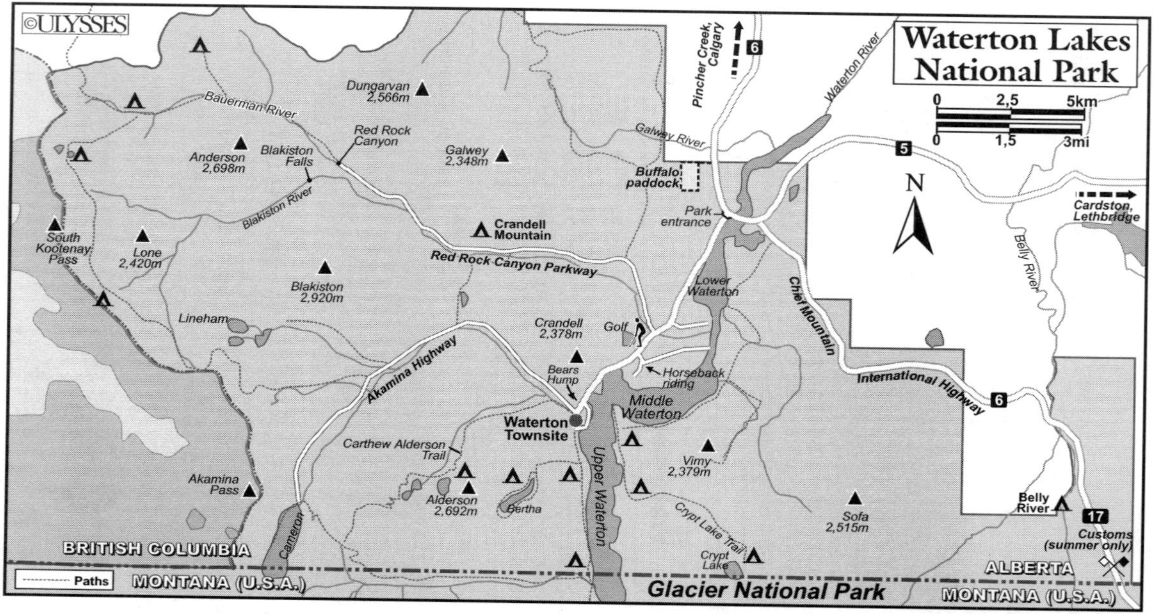
©ULYSSES
Waterton Lakes National Park
0 2,5 5km
0 1,5 3mi
N
Pincher Creek, Calgary
6
Waterton River
Galwey River
5
Cardston, Lethbridge
Belly River
Buffalo paddock
Park entrance
Dungarvan 2,566m
Bauerman River
Red Rock Canyon
Anderson 2,698m
Blakiston Falls
Galwey 2,348m
Blakiston River
Crandell Mountain
South Kootenay Pass
Lone 2,420m
Red Rock Canyon Parkway
Blakiston 2,920m
Lower Waterton
Chief Mountain
Lineham
Crandell 2,378m
Golf
Horseback riding
Bears Hump
Akamina Highway
Middle Waterton
International Highway
Waterton Townsite
Carthew Alderson Trail
Upper Waterton
Vimy 2,379m
Akamina Pass
Alderson 2,692m
Bertha
Crypt Lake Trail
Sofa 2,515m
Belly River
17
Customs (summer only)
Cameron
Crypt Lake
BRITISH COLUMBIA
ALBERTA
Paths
MONTANA (U.S.A.)
Glacier National Park
MONTANA (U.S.A.)

The Lodge at Waterton Lakes
$165
ℜ, ≈, △, ☉, K, tv
corner of Windflower and Cameron Falls Dr.
Box 4, T0K 2M0
☎(403) 859-2151
☎800-985-6343
≠(403) 859-2229

The Lodge at Waterton Lakes is a new resort hotel in the townsite of Waterton Park. Completed in 1998, the complex has 80 rooms in nine two-storey buildings as well as 20 additional rooms affiliated with the YHA youth-hostel network. Each of the nine buildings has a theme (such as forests, lakes, birds) while the individual rooms are named and decorated accordingly. There are nature-education programs and a health spa. Some rooms have kitchenettes, whirlpool baths and fireplaces.

Prince of Wales Hotel
$175-$190
economy room
$347 suite
ℜ
Waterton Lakes National Park, T0K 2M0
☎(403) 859-2231
☎(602) 207-6000
≠(403) 859-2630
reservations:
☎236-3400

The venerable Prince of Wales Hotel, open from mid-May until the end of September, is definitely the grandest place to stay in Waterton. It features bellhops in kilts and high tea in Valerie's Tea Room, not to mention the unbeatable view. The lobby and rooms are all adorned with original wood panelling. The rooms are actually quite small and unspectacular, however, with tiny bathrooms and a rustic feel. Those on the third floor and higher have balconies. Try to request a room facing the lake which is, after all, the reason that people stay here. Things will certainly change here if the rumours about expanding the Prince of Wales are true. The atmosphere at the **Garden Court Dining Room** (*$$$$*) is unbeatable. This formal dining room serves a complete menu and daily specials that often include delicious seafood or pasta. Reservations are not accepted. Enjoying an equally elegant ambience and a stunning view also in the Prince of Wales are the **Windsor Lounge** and **Valerie's Tea Room** where afternoon tea and continental breakfast are both served.

Borderline
$
305 Windflower Ave.
☎(403) 859-2284

Borderline is a friendly place for a hearty breakfast. The home-made soups and breads are delicious. Take-out lunches are available. The place stays busy throughout the day, both inside and outside on the terrace. A section of the bookstore was converted into the coffee shop, creating a particularly pleasant atmosphere.

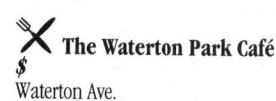

✕ The Waterton Park Café
$

Waterton Ave.

The Waterton Park Café is popular with the seasonal workers in the park as a place to eat and drink. Good sandwiches and lunch fare.

Fort Macleod

🛏 The Red Coat Inn
$40-$50

K, ≈, ®, tv

359 Col. Macleod Blvd. or Main St., Fort Macleod, T0L 0Z0

☎ *(403) 553-4434*

The Red Coat Inn is one of the most reliable motel choices in Fort Macleod. Clean, pleasant rooms, kitchenettes and a pool make this a good deal.

🛏 The Mackenzie House Bed and Breakfast
$55

1623 Third Ave., Fort Macleod, T0L 0Z0

☎/≠ *553-3302*

The Mackenzie House is located in a historic house built in 1904 for an Alberta member of the legislature at the time the province was founded in 1905. Tea and coffee are served in the afternoon, and guests are greeted in the morning with a delicious home-made breakfast.

✕ The Silver Grill
$

24th St. between Second and Third Ave.

☎ *(403) 553-3888*

The Silver Grill is an interesting alternative to the fast food joints near the motels. This historic saloon serves a mediocre Chinese buffet called a "Smorg," and typical North American dishes. It is the interior, however, that makes it worth a stop. The original bar and a bullet-pierced mirror will make you feel like you should be watching your back!

Okotoks

✕ Ginger Tea Room and Gift Shop
$-$$

43 Riverside Dr.

☎ *(403) 938-2907*

Ginger Tea Room and Gift Shop is a fanciful mix of sensible lunch fare and two floors of unique antiques and gifts. The menu includes sandwiches, soups, salads and an afternoon country tea with hot biscuits and jam. You can eat in or

La P'tite Table
$$
52 N. Railway St.
☎ *(403) 938-2224*
www.la-ptite-table.com

La P'tite Table is so *petite* that reservations are a must. The chef once cooked at the Palliser and at La Chaumiere in Calgary. Classic bistro-style French cuisine and Alberta ingredients, including duck and ostrich, are served. Perfect pastries and coffee finish the soiree.

Loon

Longview

Memories Inn
$-$$
Main St., Longview
☎ *(403) 558-3665*

Memories Inn has been decorated with the props left behind from the filming of the Clint Eastwood film *Unforgiven*. The atmosphere can get rowdy, especially during the weekend buffets which feature, among other things, succulent ribs, burgers and home-made pies.

Lethbridge

Art Deco Heritage House B&B
$50 bkfst incl.
sb
1115 Eighth Ave. S, T1J 1P7
☎ *(403) 328-3824*
≠ *(403) 328-9011*

Built in 1937, the Art Deco Heritage House B&B is located on one of Lethbridge's pretty tree-lined residential streets that's only a few minutes' walk from downtown. The guest rooms are uniquely decorated in accordance with the design of the house and include many of the house's original features. This house is an Alberta Provincial Historic Resource.

London Road B&B
$65
pb/sb
637 Ninth St. S, T1J 2L5
☎ *(403) 381-2580*
fitzpatrick@uleth.ca

London Road B&B is a friendly place just a few blocks from downtown. The rooms are very prettily decorated with iron beds, lace and floral motifs, and duvet bedspreads. Guests are made to feel very welcome with full access to the kitchen, a lounge with a fireplace and a pretty backyard and terrace. Breakfasts are copious to say the least and might feature fruit

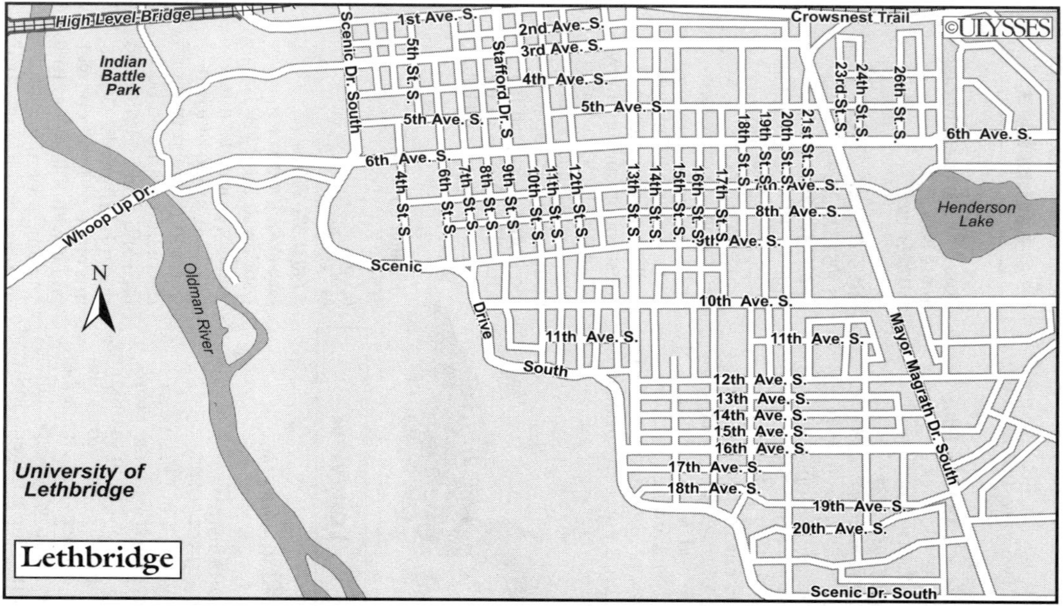
Lethbridge
©ULYSSES
High Level Bridge
Crowsnest Trail
Indian Battle Park
University of Lethbridge
Oldman River
Whoop Up Dr.
Henderson Lake
Mayor Magrath Dr. South
Scenic Dr. South
Scenic Drive South
Stafford Dr. S
N
1st Ave. S.
2nd Ave. S.
3rd Ave. S.
4th Ave. S.
5th Ave. S.
6th Ave. S.
8th Ave. S.
10th Ave. S.
11th Ave. S.
12th Ave. S.
13th Ave. S.
14th Ave. S.
15th Ave. S.
16th Ave. S.
17th Ave. S.
18th Ave. S.
19th Ave. S.
20th Ave. S.
4th St. S.
5th St. S.
6th St. S.
7th St. S.
8th St. S.
9th St. S.
10th St. S.
11th St. S.
12th St. S.
13th St. S.
14th St. S.
15th St. S.
16th St. S.
17th St. S.
18th St. S.
19th St. S.
20th St. S.
21st St. S.
23rd St. S.
24th St. S.
26th St. S.

Lethbridge

salad, muffins, crab quiche or crispy bacon. No smoking.

🛏 Days Inn
$64-$67 bkfst. incl.
≡, ⊛, K, ≈, ⊙, tv, ✈, ♿
100 Third Ave. S, T1J 4L2
☎ *(403) 327-6000*
☎ *800-661-8085*
≈ *(403) 320-2070*

Days Inn is the best motel choice downtown. The typical motel-style rooms are non-descript, but modern and clean. A free continental breakfast is served. Coin laundry available. You can also take advantage of the brand new pool.

🛏 Bartlett House B&B
$75
sb
318 12th St. S, T1J 2R1
☎ *(403) 328-4832*

Bartlett House B&B is set in a large 1910 house with red shutters. Louise, your hostess, is originally from Québec. A few of the pieces of pine furniture, along with some of the art, come from her native province. At the top of the charmingly creaky stairs, one guest room has a gorgeous antique bed and the bathroom has a lovely antique tub. Breakfast might be an Italian omelette with sausage, a baked apple pancake or a fruity biscuit, each accompanied by freshly made cappuccino. There is wine and cheese upon arrival while evening meals are available if requested ahead of time.

🛏 The Best Western Heidelberg Inn
$77-$80
≡, △, ℜ, bar, tv
1303 Mayor Magrath Dr. S, T1K 2R1
☎ *(403) 329-0555*
☎ *800-791-8488*
☎ *800-528-1234*
≈ *(403) 328-8846*

The Best Western Heidelberg Inn is an inexpensive, reliable option along the motel strip south of the city. Though the decor is a bit dated, the rooms are spotless, the staff is friendly and you get a complimentary newspaper in the morning.

🛏 Sandman Inn
$80
≡, ≈, ℜ, △, tv
421 Mayor Magrath Dr. S, T1J 3L8
☎ *(403) 328-1111*
☎ *800-726-3626*
≈ *(403) 329-9488*

The Sandman Inn is another safe bet with a nice indoor pool and clean, modern rooms.

🛏 ✕ Lethbridge Lodge Hotel
$119-$139
≡, ≈, ℜ, ⊛, tv, ✈
320 Scenic Dr., T1J 4B4
☎ *(403) 328-1123*
☎ *800-661-1232*
≈ *(403) 328-0002*

The best hotel accommodation in Lethbridge is found

at the Lethbridge Lodge Hotel overlooking the river valley. The comfortable rooms, decorated in warm and pleasant colours, seem almost luxurious when you consider the reasonable price. The rooms surround an interior tropical courtyard where small footbridges lead from the pool to the lounge and **Anton's (*$$$$*)**, the city's finest restaurant. The pasta dishes are particularly well received, as is the setting, in the hotel's tropical indoor courtyard. Reservations are recommended. **The Garden Café (*$$*)** is a less expensive alternative that is open from 6:30am to 11:30pm. Featured are hearty breakfasts and truly divine desserts.

✕ O'Sho Japanese Restaurant
$
1219 Third Ave. S
☎*(403) 327-8382*
For a change from Alberta beef, try the O'Sho Japanese Restaurant where classic Japanese fare is enjoyed in traditional style from low tables set in partitioned rooms.

✕ The Penny Coffee House
$
Fifth St. S, at 4th Ave. S
☎*(403) 320-5282*
Located next to B. Maccabee's bookseller, The Penny Coffee House is the perfect place to enjoy a good book. Don't worry if you haven't got one, there is plenty of interesting reading material on the walls. This café serves delicious hearty soups and chilis, filling sandwiches, a wonderful cheese and tomato scone, sodas and of course a great cup of Java.

✕ Cupper's
$
309A Fifth St. S
☎/≠*(403) 380-4555*
The Penny Coffee House just opened another café in the municipal library. The expansion didn't stop there. If you want to buy coffee or tea, the owner recently opened Cupper's, a little café where they roast and grind their own coffee beans. Coffees from all over the world are available.

✕ Coco Pazzo
$$
1249 Third Ave. S
☎*(403) 329-8979*
The hip Mediterranean decor at Coco Pazzo certainly has something to do with this new Italian café's success, but so does the food. The Strascinati sauce, a tomato cream sauce of their own invention, is good, though not too original. It nicely compliments the veal with capicollo in the Modo Mio dish. The vegetarian pizza is truly a veggie-lover's dream. Another house

specialty is fettuccine del Pescatore that's prepared with scallops, clams and tiger prawns.

✘ Showdowns Eatin' Adventures
$$
329 Fifth St. S
☎ *(403) 329-8830*

Showdowns Eatin' Adventures is indeed an adventure with a gun-toting, can-can-girl act. Steaks and ribs figure prominently on the menu which is rather ordinary.

✘ Shanghaï
$$
610 Third Ave. S
☎ *(403) 327-3552*

Despite an interior that could use a little freshening up, the Shanghaï restaurant offers a complete Chinese menu. They also serve North American fare (club sandwiches, hamburgers, and the like). The chicken dishes are the chef's speciality.

✘ Sven Ericksen's
$$-$$$
1714 Mayor Magrath Dr. S
☎ *(403) 328-7756*

Sven Ericksen's is a family-style restaurant that stands out among the endless fast-food joints on Mayor Magrath Drive. This restaurant has been in business since 1948, serving carefully prepared home-made dishes. The vast menu will please everyone.

Medicine Hat

▇ Groves B&B
$45 bkfst incl.
Box 998, T1A 7H1
☎ *(403) 529-6065*

Groves B&B is located about 10km (6.2mi) from downtown Medicine Hat in a peaceful spot near the South Saskatchewan River. Breakfast, which includes home-made bread, can be taken on the deck outside. There are also walking trails nearby. From downtown take Holsom Road west, turn left on Range Road 70, drive 3.3km (2.1mi) and turn right on Highway 130.

▇ The Sunny Holme B&B
$65 bkfst incl.
271 1st St. SE, T1A 0A3
☎ *526-5846*

Besides the one central hotel, there is actually another, very pleasant place to stay that is close to downtown, along pretty First Street SE. The Sunny Holme B&B is in a grand western Georgian house with a Victorian interior. The three rooms are decorated in the arts and crafts style with each having its own bathroom. A large leafy lot surrounds the house. Sourdough pancakes are just one of the breakfast

94 Southern Alberta

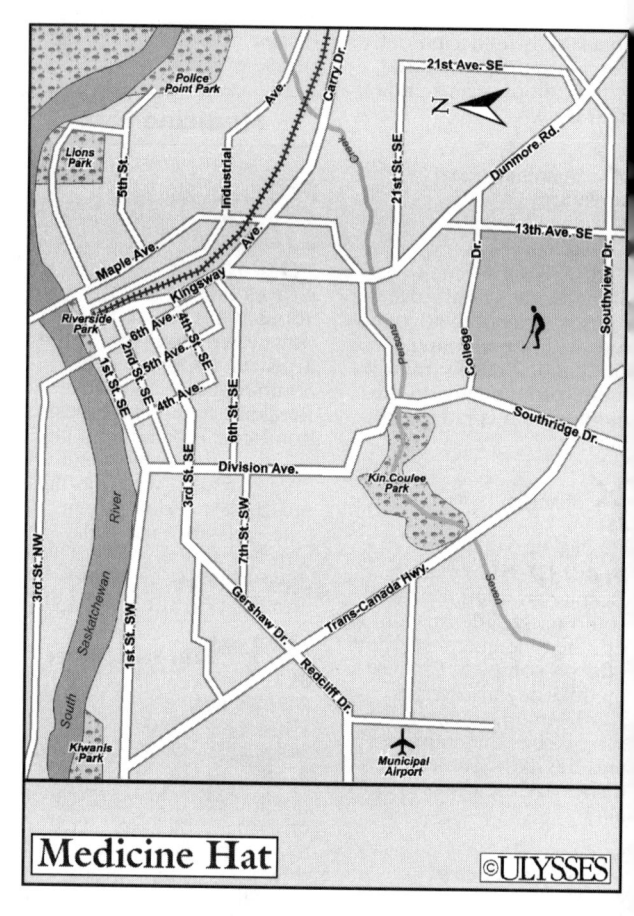

Medicine Hat

possibilities. Be sure to call ahead.

The Inn on Fourth
$56-$65
≡, ℜ, tv
530 Fourth St. SE, T1A 0K8
☎*(403) 526-1313*
☎*800-730-3887*
⇌*(403) 526-4189*

The only hotel right downtown is the little The Inn on Fourth with only 34 rooms. The rooms are clean and the hotel was completely renovated in 1997.

Medicine Hat Lodge
$79 bkfst incl.
tv, ≈, ≡, ℜ, ⊛, pb
1051 Ross Glen Dr. SE
T1B 3T8
☎*(403) 529-2222*
☎*800-661-8095*
⇌*(403) 529-1538*

Medicine Hat Lodge offers good value for the money. The rooms are standard but surprisingly pleasant with classic dark-wood furniture and pretty bedspreads. Some have sofas and all have coffee machines and hair-dryers. The hotel also has a waterslide to keep the kids happy. Its restaurant is recommended. **Mamma's Restaurant** (*$$-$$$*) offers a varied menu that features fine Alberta steaks and several pasta dishes. The food is recommended, but unfortunately the noise and chlorine smell from the hotel's waterslides is a little distracting.

Best Western Inn
$99
ℜ, ☺, ≡, ≈, △, ⊛, K, tv, ✖;
1051 Ross Glen Dr.
☎*(403) 529-2222*
⇌*(403) 529-1538*

For about the same price, you can stay along the motel strip at the Best Western Inn where the surroundings may not be as pleasant, but the facilities and rooms are more modern. Guests have access to an indoor pool and laundry facilities, and can benefit (hopefully) from the only casino in town.

The City Bakery
$
Fifth Ave. SW, between Third and Fourth St. SW
☎*(403) 527-2800*

The City Bakery bakes up wonderful fresh breads and New York bagels.

At Damon Lane's Tearoom
$
10am to 4pm, closed Mon
730 Third St. SE
☎*(403) 529-2224*

At Damon Lane's Tearoom, you can lunch on simple soups, salads and sandwiches, all home-made on the premises, or just stop in for a spot of tea and a bit of shopping. There are crafts, pottery, and decorative items for the home plus a small collection of antiques for sale.

✕ Rustler's
$

901 Eighth St. SW
☎ *(403) 526-8004*

Rustler's is another spot that transports you back to the lawless wild west; the restaurant boasts a blood-stained card table preserved under glass for all to gawk at! The menu features steaks, chicken, ribs, pasta and several Mexican dishes. Breakfasts are particularly busy and copious.

✕ Caroline's Pub & Eatery
$-$$

101 Fourth Ave. SE
☎ *(403) 529-5300*

For lunch, try Caroline's Pub & Eatery. It's a big, airy place that lacks ambience but serves good, inexpensive food.

Central Alberta

Alberta is renowned for its "big sky"– some say that nowhere is it bigger than in central Alberta.

The region encompasses a large section of land, stretching from the Alberta Heartland to the Rocky Mountains Forest Reserve. Split in two by the Red Deer River Valley, it is an area of huge, open areas of farmland and intermittent towns and cities. Red Deer is the largest centre along with the smaller towns of Camrose, Drumheller, Stettler, Wainwright and Vegreville. Most of the population there makes its living off of Alberta's bountiful natural resources.

Besides being the cradle of European settlement in Alberta, this is also where a large number of dinosaur bones have been discovered, preserved for millions of years under the surface of the earth. The region's Badlands contain fossil beds of international significance – over 300 complete dinosaur skeletons have been found here. Every time it rains in the Red Deer River Valley, more bones are discovered.

Still, one of central Alberta's most appealing attractions is the view at night from its prairies. Here, it is possible to get lost in the "big sky" and to feel truly alone with a billion stars.

Accommodations

The small towns sprinkled between Rocky Mountain House and Drumheller in central Alberta generally offer two tiers of accommodation. Many unremarkable "bare bones" motor inns cater to both tourists and the transient nature of workers in Alberta's natural resource industries. There is also a fair share of surprisingly charming inns and bed and breakfasts, many of which feature the pioneer style of Old West manors and ranches. Appealingly rustic, these places can take you back to an era when the West was still being settled and pioneers had to work the land to survive.

Restaurants

While exotic international cuisine is available in a few establishments in places with higher tourist traffic, you should probably wait for a restaurant in Calgary or Edmonton to satisfy your craving. If you want to fill up on hearty country cuisine, there are countless choices throughout the region. Breakfast could become your favourite meal of the day with huge rancher's breakfasts available in many places. Later in the day, thick soups, sandwich lunches and Alberta-beef steaks and burgers are mainstays.

Many of the area's inhabitants are descendants of Ukrainian immigrants who settled in the region which has many restaurants offering excellent Ukrainian cuisine. Borscht and perogies could be the perfect alternative to the omnipresent Alberta beef.

Brooks

Tel-Star Motor Inn
$56
ℜ, ≡, ℝ, K, tv
813 Second St. W., on the way into town, Box 547, T1R 1B5
☎ *(403) 362-3466*
☎ *800-260-6211*
≠ *(403) 362-8818*

About 30min down the highway from Dinosaur Provincial Park is the town of Brooks and the Tel-Star Motor Inn. The rooms don't have much to recommend them aside from the fact that they are clean and each has a microwave and a refrigerator. The hotel also doesn't charge for local calls and has freezer facilities for your catch.

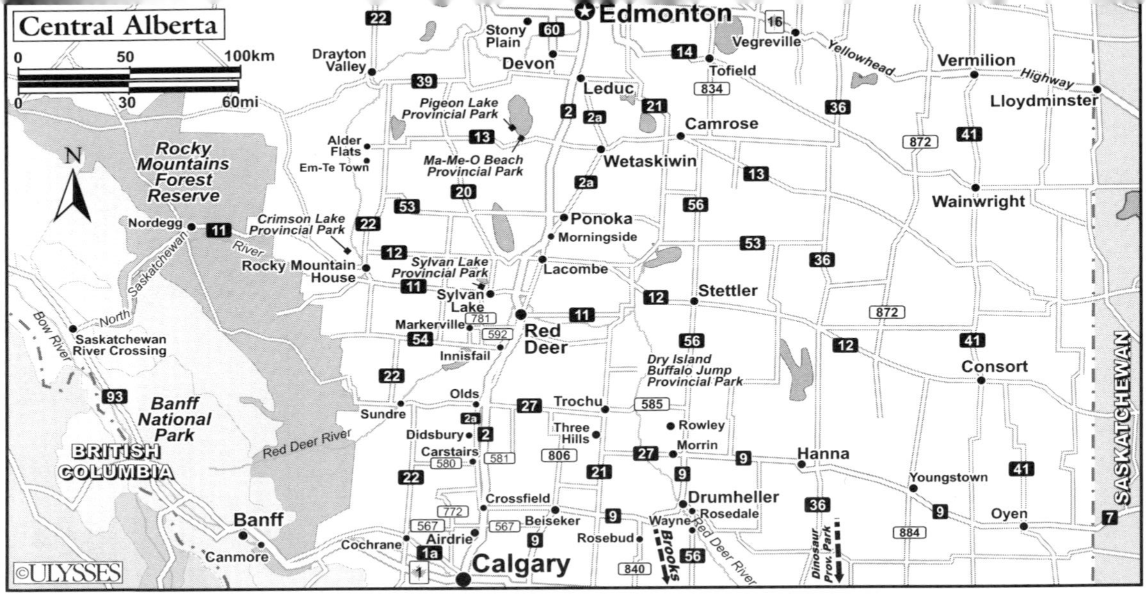
Central Alberta
0
50
100km
0
30
60mi
N
Edmonton
Stony Plain
Devon
Leduc
Drayton Valley
Vegreville
Tofield
Yellowhead Highway
Vermilion
Lloydminster
Pigeon Lake Provincial Park
Ma-Me-O Beach Provincial Park
Camrose
Wetaskiwin
Alder Flats
Em-Te Town
Rocky Mountains Forest Reserve
Wainwright
Nordegg
Crimson Lake Provincial Park
Ponoka
Morningside
North Saskatchewan River
Rocky Mountain House
Lacombe
Sylvan Lake Provincial Park
Sylvan Lake
Stettler
Red Deer
Markerville
Innisfail
Saskatchewan River Crossing
Bow River
Dry Island Buffalo Jump Provincial Park
Consort
Banff National Park
Olds
Trochu
Sundre
Didsbury
Three Hills
Rowley
Morrin
Carstairs
Hanna
Red Deer River
BRITISH COLUMBIA
Crossfield
Beiseker
Drumheller
Rosedale
Wayne
Youngstown
Oyen
Airdrie
Rosebud
Brooks
Dinosaur Prov. Park
Banff
Canmore
Cochrane
Calgary
SASKATCHEWAN
©ULYSSES

100 Central Alberta

🛶 🛏 Douglas Country Inn
$77 bkfst incl.
ℜ, ≡, pb
Box 463, T1R 1B5
☎ *(403) 362-2873*
≠ *(403) 362-2100*

The Douglas Country Inn is 6.5km (4mi) north of town on Highway 873. A casual country atmosphere is achieved in each of the seven beautifully appointed rooms and throughout the rest of the inn. The only television is in the small TV room which is rarely used. Enjoy your complimentary sherry by the fire in the sitting room. The special occasion room *($99)* boasts a divine Japanese soaker tub with a view.

✗ Peggy Sue's Diner
$
603 Second St. W

Peggy Sue's is a neat little family-run eatery. Smoked meat, burgers, great fries and delicious mud pie can be eaten in or taken out.

Drumheller

🛏 Badlands Motel
$60
≡, ℜ, ℝ, K, tv
on the Dinosaur Trail
Box 2217, T0J 0Y0
☎ *(403) 823-5155*
≠ *(403) 823-7653*

The Badlands Motel lies outside of town along the scenic Dinosaur Trail. Rooms are typical, but the pancake restaurant next door is particularly noteworthy.

🛏 Waldorf Hotel
$25-$30
pb
70 Railview Ave.
☎ *(403) 823-6687*
☎ *(403) 823-2623*

The Waldorf Hotel is in one of the oldest buildings in Drumheller. And it shows! While the rooms are adequate, they are in deplorable condition and smell musty. As for the decor, it isn't memorable – but the price is.

🛏 Newcastle Country Inn
$80 bkfst incl.
≡
1130 Newcastle Trail
☎ *(403) 823-8356*

The Newcastle Country Inn offers decently decorated, comfortable rooms. The breakfasts are filling and the staff is friendly. The plumbing, however, is sometimes noisy.

🛶 🛏 Taste the Past B&B
$79
sb, ⊗
281 Second St. W. Box 865, T0J 0Y0
☎ *(403) 823-5889*

The fittingly named Taste the Past B&B is a 1910 Victorian house decorated with antiques. Guests enjoy a large yard and veranda and a choice of breakfasts. They also have the use of a warm bathrobe and slippers. In 1998, this establishment went from four to three rooms, giving its guests more privacy. Each room now has its own private bathroom.

Heartwood Manor
$79-$150
⊛, ≡, tv, ✻, ♿
320 Railway Ave. E, T0J 0Y4
☎ *(403) 823-6495*
☎ *888-823-6495*
⇌ *(403) 823-4935*

By far the prettiest place to stay in town is the Heartwood Manor, a bed and breakfast in a restored heritage building where a striking use of colour creates a cozy and luxurious atmosphere. Nine of the ten rooms have whirlpool baths with five even featuring fireplaces. A spacious cottage and a two-bedroom suite are also available. Yummy home-made fruit syrups are served with the pancake breakfast. French and English spoken.

Best Western Jurassic Inn
$89-$129
≡, ≈, ⊛, ℜ
1103 Hwy. 9 S, T0J 0Y0
☎ *(403) 823-7700*
☎ *800-528-1234*
⇌ *(403) 823-5002*

The Best Western has 49 guest rooms. They are standard, but very clean and very well equipped with a fridge, microwave and hair dryer. Continental breakfast is included.

The Corner Stop Restaurant
$$
15 Third Ave. W
☎ *(403) 823-5440*

The Corner Stop Restaurant is located in the middle of the city. With a meticulous Greek-style decor, the menu includes salads, pizza, pasta, seafood and steaks.

Yavis Family Restaurant
$$
249 Third Ave.
☎ *(403) 823-8317*

This restaurant has been around for years. The interior is fairly non-descript, and so is the menu. The selections are nonetheless pretty good, especially the great big breakfasts.

The Bridge
$$
71 Bridge St. N
☎ *(403) 823-2225*

The Bridge is a Greek restaurant that serves a bit of everything, including steaks and pasta dishes. While they are a bit on the greasy side, the Greek selections are the best, coming in huge portions with tsatziki on the side (i.e. don't order more!). With a recently redone interior and the Greek background music, it is faintly reminiscent of the Mediterranean.

Sizzling House
$$
160 Centre St.
☎(403) 823-8098
The Sizzling House serves up tasty Thai cooking, that is recommended by locals. A good place for lunch, the service is quick and friendly.

Trochu

St. Ann Ranch
$55-$75
Box 670, T0M 2C0
☎(403) 442-3924
Once the ranch of French cavalry men, the St. Ann Ranch country bed and breakfast offers travellers the chance to experience a true French *gîte*. Guests of the B&B have the choice of seven private, antique-furnished rooms (five with private baths) in the rambling 30-room ranch house or in the Pioneer Cottage and the use of a parlour with a fireplace, a library and patios. While you're here visit the tea house and museum.

Rosebud

Rosebud Country Inn
$95
pb, ♿, no smoking
Box 631, T0J 2T0
☎(403) 677-2211
≠(403) 677-2106
Rooms at the Rosebud Country Inn feature queen-size sleigh beds, designer linens, pedestal sinks and balconies. Roses brighten up the interior space throughout. This inn boasts first-rate facilities and spotless accommodations. The tea room serves breakfast, Sunday brunch, lunch, supper and, of course, afternoon tea. The inn organizes murder-mystery packages in the winter. There are no televisions (by choice) and children are not permitted.

American Robin

The Rosebud Dinner Theatre is an entertaining way to spend an evening. While the food is simple, the plays are always well presented. Reservations are mandatory; for schedules and information call **☎(403) 677-2001 or 800-267-7553**.

The region's largest city, Red Deer, hosts a great number of conventions year-round. As a result, weekend rates in its many hotels are often less expensive than during the rest of the week. Unfortunately, Red Deer's hotels are for the most part your run-of-the-mill variety, but comfortable nonetheless.

Cochrane

Dickens Inn
$75-$85 bkfst incl.
R.R. 1, T0L 0W0
2km west of Cochrane on the 1A, turn right on Horse Creek Rd. and continue for 7km, driveway to the right
☎ *(403) 932-3945*

Take in the panoramic views of the mountains from the Dickens Inn, a Victorian house built as a B&B. Enjoy peaceful slumber in one of three guest rooms with queen-size four-poster beds and private bathrooms. Then guests awaken to a copious breakfast featuring home-made preserves and fresh bread.

Mackay's Ice Cream
$
☎ *(403) 932-2455*

Mackay's Ice Cream scoops up what many claim is the best ice cream in the country. Be sure to stop in to see for yourself!

Home Quarter Restaurant & Pie Shoppe
$$
216 First St. W
☎ *(403) 932-2111*

Cochrane's friendly Home Quarter Restaurant is the home of the ever-popular Rancher's Special breakfast with eggs, bacon and sausage. Home-made pies are available all day long to eat in or take out. The lunch and dinner menu includes filet mignon and chicken parmesan.

Sylvan Lake

Sylvan Lake Bed & Breakfast
$50 bkfst incl.
tv, sb
3723 50th Ave., T4S 1B5
☎ *(403) 887-3546*

The Sylvan Lake B&B is run by a globetrotting couple who speak English, Swedish, Spanish and Portuguese. The rooms are simple yet intimate, while outside the lovely yard is very peaceful. Only one block from the beach. For $60 you can have a suite with an extra room as well as a sofa and television.

Rocky Mountain House

🛏 Voyageur Motel
$58
≡, *K*, ℝ, *tv*
on Hwy. 11 S, Box 1376, T0M 1T0
☎ *(403) 845-3381*
☎ *888-845-3569*
⇌ *(403) 845-6166*

The Voyageur is a practical choice with spacious, clean rooms, each equipped with a refrigerator. Kitchenettes are also available for a surcharge. Each room has a VCR.

🛏 Walking Eagle Motor Inn
$75, cabins $35
≡, ℜ, *tv, bar, fridge*
on Hwy. 11, Box 1317, T0M 1T0
☎ *(403) 845-2804*
⇌ *(403) 845-3685*

The log exterior of the Walking Eagle Motor Inn encloses 63 clean and large rooms decorated in keeping with the hotel's name. The hotel owes its attractive appearance to a complete renovation and paint-job. In addition, a brand new 35-room motel *($80)* was built right next door. There's a microwave and refrigerator in each one of the clean – but rather drab – rooms.

Nordegg

🛏 David Thompson Resort
$70
pb, ≡, ≈
☎ *(403) 721-2103*

This is more of a motel and RV park than a resort. Regardless, it is the only accommodation between Nordegg and Highway 93, the Icefields Parkway, and you can't beat the scenery. The resort rents bicycles and can organize helicopter tours of the area.

Red Deer

Many conventions are held in Red Deer, and as a result weekend rates in the many hotels are often less expensive.

🛏 McIntosh Tea House Bed and Breakfast
$65
pb
4631 50th St., T4N 1X1
☎ *(403) 346-1622*

This is the former home of the great grandson of the creator of the McIntosh apple. Each of the three upstairs rooms of the red-brick historic Victorian is decorated with antiques. Guests can enjoy a game of apple checkers in the private parlour. Tea and coffee are served in the evening and a full breakfast in the morning.

Red Deer 105

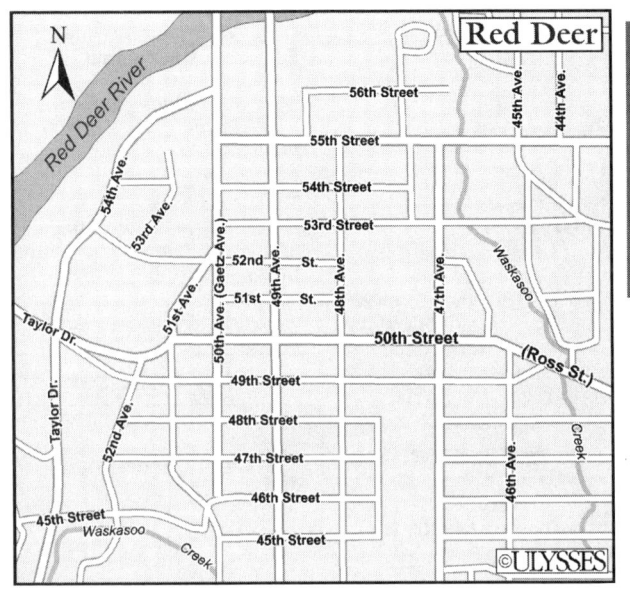

Central Alberta

Red Deer Lodge
$89-$149
≡, ≈, ℜ, *bar*, ⊛, *tv*, 🐾
4311 49th Ave., T4N 5Y7
☎ *(403) 346-8841*
☎ *800-661-1657*
≠ *(403) 341-3220*

The Red Deer Lodge is a favourite with convention-goers because of its modern and extensive amenities. As one would expect, the rooms are comfortable and spotless. The rooms surround a cheerful courtyard.

City Roast Coffee
$
4940 50th St.
☎ *(403) 347-0893*

The City Roast serves hearty soup, sandwich lunches and good coffee. The walls are decorated with posters announcing local art shows and events.

Good Food Company
$-$$
at the corner of 50th St. and Gaetz Ave.
☎ *(403) 343-8185*

This restaurant is located in the old Greene Block, a historic building in downtown Red Deer. Healthy meals including borscht and a peasant's platter are all served with home-made bread.

✗ Cheesecake Café
$$
4320 Gaetz Ave.
☎ *(403) 341-7818*
≠ *(403) 341-7849*

The Cheesecake Cafe has a vast selection of famous desserts. But there's more: a laid-back atmosphere, fast and friendly service as well as an eclectic menu. You won't regret your visit.

Wetaskiwin

🛏 The Rose Country Inn
$$$
≡, ℜ, ℝ, K, bar, tv
4820 56th St., T9A 2G5
☎ *(780) 352-3600*
≠ *(780) 352-2127*

Close to the Reynolds-Alberta Museum, on 56th Street, the Rose Country Inn is one of the best deals in town. Each of the recently renovated rooms has a refrigerator and microwave oven.

✗ The MacEachern Tea House & Restaurant
$-$$
Mon to Sat until 4:30pm, Jul and Aug also open Sun 10am to 4pm
4719 50th Ave.
☎ *(780) 352-8308*

Home to specialty coffees and over 20 teas. The menu boasts hearty home-made soups and chowders as well as sandwiches and salads.

Lloydminster

✗ Lunch at Lorna's
$-$$
5008 50th St.
☎ *(780) 875-1152*

Lorna's is a friendly spot near the downtown area. They serve simple fare like soups and sandwiches.

✗ Greek Classic
$$-$$$
4402 52nd Ave.
☎ *(780) 875-3553*

Probably the fanciest restaurant in Lloyd, though fancy might be pushing it. The menu might be small, but the food is very well prepared and nice and spicy!

Edmonton

Alberta's provincial capital was founded on the successful booms of three natural resources: fur, gold and oil.

For over 5,000 years prior to the arrival of the first Europeans, the nomadic Plains Indians occupied the area of present-day Edmonton on the North Saskatchewan River. As settlers trudged west in an effort to feed the growing fur trade, Edmonton House was established by the Hudson's Bay Company in 1795 where there was a seemingly endless supply of beaver and muskrat. Almost a century later, the Klondike gold rush brought prospectors through the area (at the time Fort Edmonton), with gold seekers looking to be outfitted before making their long drive further north to Dawson City. Unfortunately, the legendary trail between the two cities did not actually exist. Many perished in their attempts to find the route.

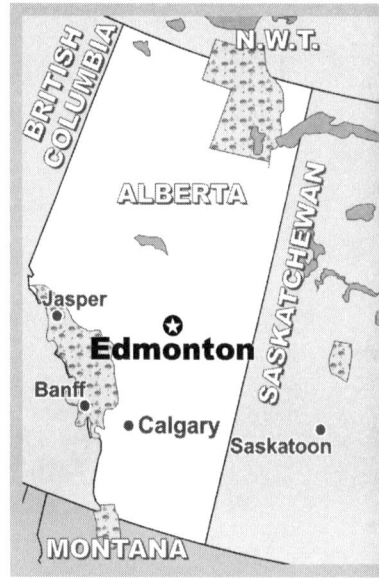

On September 1, 1905, the province of Alberta was founded. The northern outpost of Edmonton was named the capital, much to the chagrin of other growing Alberta towns such as Calgary and Banff. Later in the century, oil was found in the province, and a new

108   Edmonton

industry brought prosperity to the city. By 1965, Edmonton had become the oil capital of Canada, and the 1970s boom in oil prices brought forth a skyline of modern steel and glass towers.

Today, the city is influenced as much by the local arts community and students of the thriving University of Alberta (the second-largest university in Canada) as by the once-booming oil industry. Some corners of Edmonton have a decidedly bohemian feel. For a city known for its gargantuan shopping mall, there remain many hidden and surprising treasures.

Accommodations

Visitors to the city can choose from more than 9,000 hotels, motels and bed and breakfasts. Downtown there is a wide range international hotel chains offering comfortable, modern rooms with fairly good quality-to-price ratios. Less expensive options can be found in the city's Old Strathcona district, an historic area on the south side of Edmonton.

If you've been lured to Edmonton by the West Edmonton Mall and want to stay as close to it as possible, the Fantasyland Hotel may be what you're looking for. Located right inside the mall, the hotel offers theme rooms ranging from the bizarre to the charming, depending on your taste. Choices for rooms include an igloo, a horse-drawn coach, the back of a pickup truck and various international settings.

ACCOMMODATIONS

1. Best Western Cedar Park Inn
2. Best Western Westwood Inn
3. Edmonton West Travel Lodge
4. Fantasyland Hotel & Resort
5. Holgate House B&B
6. La Bohème B&B
7. Southbend Motel
8. West Harvest Inn

RESTAURANTS

1. Barb and Ernie's
2. Cheesecake Café Bakery Restaurant
3. La Bohème
4. Syrtaki Greek Restaurant
5. West Edmonton Mall

Edmonton
0 2.5 5km
0 1.5 3mi
N
ST. ALBERT
Boudreau Rd.
St. Albert Trail
195th Ave.
167th Ave.
153rd Ave.
137th Ave.
132nd Ave.
127th Ave.
Yellowhead Trail
118th Ave.
111th Ave.
107th Ave.
104th Ave.
Stony Plain Rd.
102nd Ave.
100th Ave.
Jasper Ave.
98th Ave.
95th Ave.
87th Ave.
Whyte Ave.
76th Ave.
Whitemud Dr.
63rd Ave.
61st Ave.
51st Ave.
34th Ave.
23rd Ave.
184th St.
170th St.
158th St.
149th St.
142nd St.
127th St.
124th St.
122nd St.
119th St.
116th St.
114th St.
113th St.
113A St.
109th St.
104th St.
103rd St.
101st St.
99th St.
97th St.
82nd St.
75th St.
66th St.
17 St.
Groat Rd.
Kingsway
Capilano Dr.
Connors Rd.
University Ave.
Buena Vista Road
Terwillegar Dr.
Calgary Trail
North Saskatchewan River
OLD STRATHCONA
See map of Edmonton Centre
Edmonton International Airport
16
28
2
©ULYSSES

If a more subdued bed and breakfast is to your liking, there are many in the city. We suggest contacting **Edmonton Bed & Breakfast** *(13824 - 110A Ave.; ☎ 780-455-2297)*.

Restaurants

Among the 2,000-odd dining locations in Edmonton, there are some 30 different international cuisines with offerings of varied cultures to be found in every corner of the city.

In close proximity to downtown's Jasper Avenue, there are a number of reasonably priced cafés that are popular with the city's arts community. On the south side of Edmonton, the Whyte Avenue district is the place to be. In close proximity to the University of Edmonton and stretching into Old Strathcona, the street's brick sidewalks and old-fashioned street lamps add a distinct charm to the area's pavement cafés and restaurants. There is excellent food to be found here.

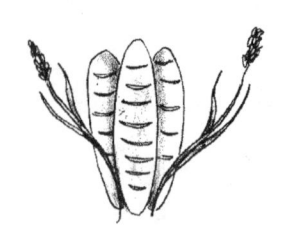

Downtown

The Days Inn Downtown
$50-$60
ℝ, ≡, ℜ, ⊛, △, *tv, bar,* 🐾
10041 106th St., T5J 1G3
☎*(780) 423-1925*
☎*800-267-2191 or 800-DAYS-INN*
⇌*(780) 424-5302*

The Days Inn Dowtown boasts comfortable, modern rooms. This is another downtown spot with a good quality to price ratio.

Grand Hotel
$51 bkfst incl.
10266 103rd St., corner of 103rd Ave.
☎*(780) 422-6365*

At the Grand Hotel you will be fascinated by Edmonton's cowboy past. With its tavern, diner, dance hall and 79 anonymous dark rooms, the Grand Hotel seems like it came right out of one of Lucky Lake's comic strips. Despite its minimal comfort and lacklustre appearance, people come here for the price and location (the Greyhound bus terminal is right across the street).

The Econo Lodge
$54-$59
P, ≡, ℜ, ⊛, *tv, bar,* 🐾
10209 100th Ave., T5J 0A1
☎*(780) 428-6442*
☎*800-613-7043*

This Econo Lodge has 73 rooms including some suites featuring whirlpool baths. Parking and an air-

Inn on Seventh
$70
≡, ℜ, ⊛, tv, bar, ☺, ✈
10001 107th St., T5J 1J1
☎ *(780) 429-2861*
☎ *800-661-7327*
≠ *(780) 426-7225*

Fifteen of the nearly 200 clean and modern rooms at the Inn on Seventh are "environmentally safe," though this just means they are non-smoking rooms on non-smoking floors. Weekend rates are available. Facilities include coin-laundry machines.

Best Western City Centre
$89-$99
≡, ≈, ℜ, ⊛, tv, bar, △
11310 109th St., T5G 2T7
☎ *(780) 479-2042*
☎ *800-666-5026*
☎ *800-528-1234*
≠ *(780) 474-2204*

This Best Western is not quite in the city centre and has a rather dated exterior. The rooms are nevertheless very comfortable and pleasantly decorated with wooden furniture.

port shuttle service make this a good deal for those looking for lodging downtown. Rooms are nothing special, however.

Alberta Suite Hotel
$90-$110
tv, ⊛, K, ≡, ☺, △, ⊛
10049 102nd Street, near Jasper Avenue
☎ *(780) 423-1565*
☎ *(780) 800 661-3982*
≠ *(780) 426-6260*
www.albertaplace.com

As the name indicates, the Alberta Suite Hotel offers mini-apartments with kitchenettes and work areas. With its friendly staff and unpretentious, tastefully decorated rooms, this establishment is a perfect compromise between impersonal, luxury hotels and budget accommodation.

Edmonton Westin Hotel
$115-$155
≈, ≡, ℜ
10135 100th St.
☎ *(780) 426-3636*
≠ *(780) 428-1454*
www.westin.ab.ca

The Edmonton Westin Hotel was built on the site of the first post office in the city. This modern facility with 413 rooms is located in what is now the heart of the business district. The guests, mostly from the business district, enjoy the restaurant, pool and enormous terrace – all of which exude luxury.

Union Bank Inn Hotel
$125-$165, bkfst
≡, ⊛, ℜ; 10053 Jasper Avenue, between 100th and 101st Sts.
☎ *(780) 423-3600*
☎ *888-423-3601*
⇌ *(780) 423-4623*
www.unionbank.com

The Union Bank, constructed in 1910, was the first bank built on Jasper Street. Relegated to pigeons and the homeless, it was transformed into the Union Bank Inn Hotel after a major facelift in 1997. Each of the 14 magnificent and inviting rooms is the work of a different decorator. Every room has a fireplace and a whirlpool. The delicious **Madison Grill ($$$)** is on the main floor. The dining room is as impeccably decorated as the rooms. Its high quality food from the four corners of the globe has earned it a place among the top 100 restaurants in the country.

The Edmonton House Suite Hotel
$140-$195
ℜ, K, ≈, △, tv, ☺, ✖
10205 100th Ave., T5J 4B5
☎ *(780) 420-4000*
☎ *800-661-6562*
⇌ *(780) 420-4008*

The Edmonton House is actually an apartment-hotel

○ ACCOMMODATIONS	● RESTAURANTS
1. Alberta Suite Hotel	1. Bagel Tree
2. Best Western City Centre	2. Baraka Café
3. Commercial Hotel	3. Bee-Bell Health Bakery
4. Days Inn Downtown	4. Bistro Praha
5. Delta Edmonton Centre Suite Hotel	5. Block 1912
6. Econo Lodge	6. Café Select
7. Edmonton International Hostel	7. Chianti Café
8. Edmonton Westin Hotel	8. Claude's on the River
9. Grand Hotel	9. Funky Pickle Pizza co.
10. Hotel Macdonald	10. Hy's Steakloft
11. Inn on Seventh	11. Julio's Barrio
12. Strathcona Hotel	12. Levis by the River
13. The Edmonton House Suite Hotel	13. Madison Grill
14. Union Bank Inn Hotel	14. Manifesto
15. Varscona	15. Pacific Fish
	16. Packrat Louie Kitchen & Bar
	17. Plantier's
	18. Symposium
	19. The Unheardof Restaurant
	20. Turtle Creek

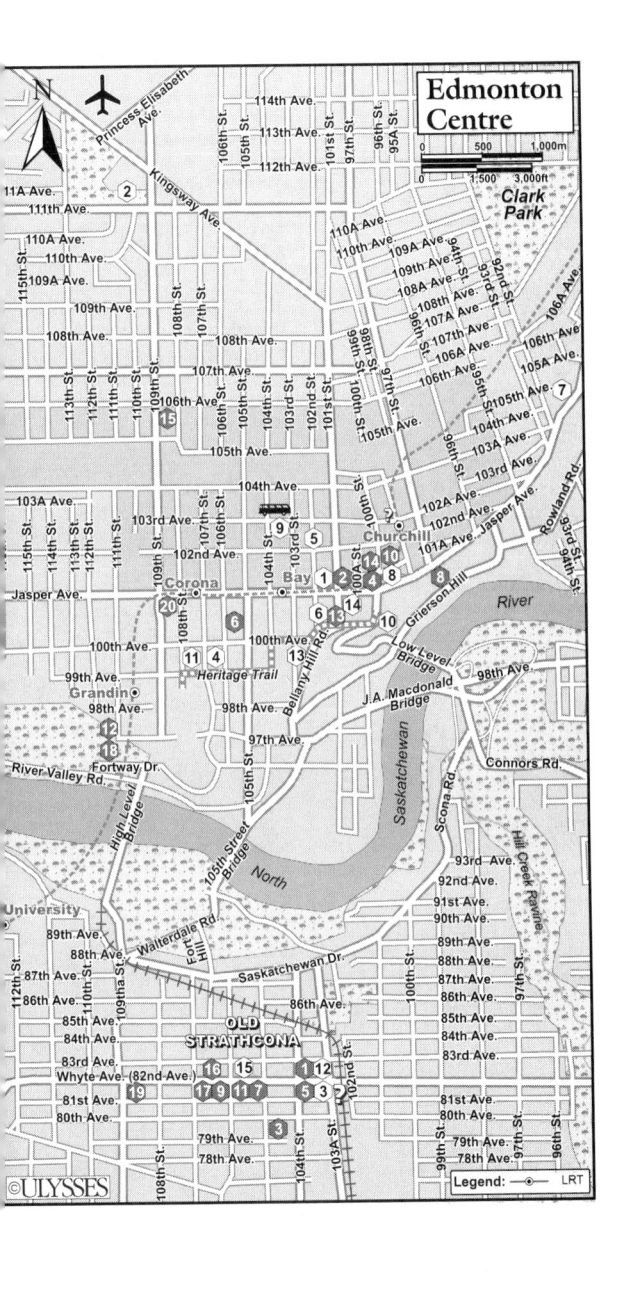

Edmonton Centre

with suites that features kitchens and balconies. This is one of the better apartment-hotel options in town. Reservations are recommended.

🛏 Delta Edmonton Centre Suite Hotel
$154-$220
ℜ, ⊛, △, *tv, bar*, ≡, ☉, 🐕
10222 102nd St., T5J 4C5
☎ *(780) 429-3900*
☎ *800-661-6655*
⇌ *(780) 426-0562*

This Delta is part of the downtown Eaton Centre shopping mall. Apart from the hotel's extensive facilities, this means that guests have access to shops and cinemas. Rooms are comfortable and the suites are lavishly decorated.

🌴 🛏 Hotel MacDonald
$249-$295
≡, ℜ, ≈, ⊛, △, ☉, *tv, bar*, 🐕, ♿
10065 100th St., T5J 0N6
☎ *(780) 424-5181*
☎ *800-441-1414*
⇌ *(780) 424-8017*
www.cphotels.com

Edmonton's grand chateau-style Hotel MacDonald is stunning. Classic styling from the guest rooms to the dining rooms make this an exquisite place to stay. A variety of weekend packages are available, including golf packages and romantic getaways. Call for details.

✕ Baraka Café
$
corner of Jasper Avenue and 101st St.
☎ *(780) 423-1819*

Ideally located, the Baraka Café offers a laid-back atmosphere where clients of all ages and backgrounds mingle. People come here to drink fresh juice, good coffee or bite into one of their many delicious sandwiches.

✕ Manifesto
$
10043 102nd St., near Jasper Avenue
☎ *(780) 423-7901*

An arts space, café, as well as a second-hand bookstore, Manifesto is purely underground. They serve light fare such as soup and bagels. A few large, inviting couches complete the picture. All sorts of gatherings take place here on weekends from the launching of a new CD to art expositions or a performance of video scratch.

✕ Cheesecake Café Bakery Restaurant
$
17011 100th Ave.
☎ *(780) 486-0440*
10390 51st Ave.
☎ *(780) 437-5011*

A huge variety of cheesecakes—need we say more?

Levis by the River
$
9712 111th St.
☎ (780) 482-6402

Levis is located in a converted house overlooking the North Saskatchewan River Valley. Innovative and delicious dishes are served in its several small dining rooms. In the summer on the terrace, dine while enjoying great views and spectacular sunsets. Service can be slow if they are really busy, but the chocolate pecan pie on the dessert menu is worth the wait!

The West Edmonton Mall's
Bourbon Street harbours a collection of moderately priced restaurants. **Café Orleans** *($$; ☎ 780-444-2202)* serves Cajun and Creole specialties; **Sherlock Holmes** *($$; ☎ 780-444-1752)* serves typical English pub grub; **Albert's Family Restaurant** *($; ☎ 780-444-1179)* serves Montréal-style smoked meat; the **Modern Art Café** *($-$$; ☎ 780-444-2233)* is a new-world bistro with pizzas, pasta and steaks where everything (the art, the furniture) is for sale.

Pacific Fish
$$-$$$
10020 101A Ave.
☎ (780) 422-0282

Also known as Frank's Place, this is perhaps Edmonton's best seafood restaurant with fresh fish arriving daily. Reservations are recommended.

Bistro Praha
$$$
10168 100A St.
☎ (780) 424-4218

Edmonton's first European bistro, Bistro Praha is very popular and charges accordingly. Favourites like cabbage soup, Wiener schnitzel, filet mignon, tortes and strudels are served in a refined but comfortable setting.

Café Select
$$$
10018 106th St.
☎ (780) 423-0419

The posh ambience at the Café Select is deceiving. The atmosphere is actually elegantly unpretentious which is all the better to enjoy the delicious entrées featured on the evening menu of the week. With a 2am closing time on Fridays and Saturdays, this is the place for a fashionably late meal.

Plantier's
$$$
10807 106th Ave.
☎ (780) 990-1992

Plantier's serves up flavourful French creations like spiced, roasted salmon and sublime escargots. For dessert, try delicate French pastries or their specialty,

Alberta's Legislature Building

crème brûlée. Friendly service.

✕ Claude's on the River
$$$$
9797 Jasper Ave.
☎ *(780) 429-2900*
This is one of Edmonton's finest restaurants. An exceptional river-valley view, menu offerings like Australian rack of lamb in a provençale crust and other distinguished French dishes as well as an extensive wine list explain why.

✕ Hy's Steakloft
$$$$
10013 101A Ave.
☎ *(780) 424-4444*
Like its Calgary counterpart, Hy's Steakloft serves up juicy Alberta steaks done to perfection. Chicken and pasta dishes round out the menu. A beautiful skylight is the centrepiece of the restaurant's classy decor.

West of Downtown

🛌 West Harvest Inn
$72-$79
≡, ℜ, ⊛, *tv*
17803 Stony Plain Rd., T5S 1B4
☎ *(780) 484-8000*
☎ *800-661-6993*
≠ *(780) 486-6060*
The West Harvest Inn is the other inexpensive choice within striking distance of the mall. This hotel is relatively quiet and receives quite a few business travellers.

🛌 Best Western Westwood Inn
$79
≡, △, ⊘, ≈, ℜ, *tv*
18035 Stony Plain Rd., T5S 1B2
☎ *(780) 483-7770*
☎ *800-557-4767*
☎ *800-528-1234*
≠ *(780) 486-1769*
The Best Western Westwood Inn is also close to the mall. While the rooms are more expensive here,

they are also much larger, noticeably more comfortable and more pleasantly decorated.

Edmonton West Travelodge
$79-$89
≈, ≡, ⊛, tv, 🐕
18320 Stony Plain Rd., T5S 1A7
☎ *(780) 483-6031*
☎ *800-578-7878*
≠ *(780) 484-2358*

For those who want to be close to the shopping but aren't necessarily big spenders, the Edmonton West Travelodge is one of two relatively inexpensive hotels located close to the West Edmonton Mall. The rooms were recently redone and there is a big indoor pool.

Fantasyland Hotel & Resort
$165
☺, 🐕, ≡, ℜ, ⊛, △, tv, bar
17700 87th Ave., T5T 4V4
☎ *(780) 444-3000*
☎ *800-661-6454*
≠ *(780) 444-3294*
www.fantasylandhotel.com

Travellers on a shopping vacation will certainly want to be as close to the West Edmonton Mall as possible, making the Fantasyland Hotel & Resort the obvious choice. Of course, you might also choose to stay here just for the sheer delight of spending the night under African or Arabian skies or in the back of a pick-up truck!

✗ Syrtaki Greek Restaurant
$$-$$$
16313 111th Ave.
☎ *(780) 484-2473*

The whitewashed and blue decor of the Syrtaki Greek Restaurant is enough to make you forget you are in Edmonton. Belly dancers animate the evening on Fridays and Saturdays. Fresh game, seafood, meat, chicken and vegetables are all prepared according to authentic Greek recipes.

East of Downtown

Holgate House B&B
$85
≡
6210 Ada Blvd, T5W 4P1
☎/≠ *(780) 471-1185*

The Holgate House B&B is located nearby in the historic Highlands district. It offers two exquisite rooms decorated in the "arts and crafts" style, one with private bath and the other boasting an ensuite bathroom complete with a six-foot soaker tub. After exploring the scenic streets that surround the house and overlook the Saskatchewan River Valley, guests can relax on the lovely front verandah, in the sitting room by a roaring fire or in the morning room with a good book.

La Boheme B&B
$140
K
6427 112th Ave., T5W 0N9
☎ *(780) 474-5693*
≠ *(780) 479-1871*
gecentures.com/laboheme

Set on the second floor of the historic Gibbard Building and upstairs from the restaurant of the same name, La Boheme B&B occupies the rooms of a former luxury apartment building. All the rooms are charmingly decorated and equipped with kitchenettes. However you will find it hard to resist the gastronomical delights at the restaurant (*$$$*) downstairs. A delicious variety of classic yet original French appetizers and entrées is enjoyed in a romantic setting complete with a cozy fire.

Old Strathcona

The cheaper hotels are situated in Strathcona. We found two that we liked. With its 40 rooms located in one of the oldest wooden buildings in Edmonton, the **Strathcona Hotel** (*$28; sb/pb, 10302 82nd Ave, near 103rd Street;* ☎ *780-439-1992*) is less expensive and more attractive than its neighbour across the street, the **Commercial Hotel** (*$31; sb/pb; 10329 82nd Ave.;* ☎ *780-439-3981*). It's clean and comfortable, but sometimes noisy. In both of these establishments, expect to pay extra for a private bathroom.

Varscona
$89
≡, ℜ, △, *tv, bar*
10620 Whyte Ave., T6E 2A7
☎ *(780) 434-6111*
☎ *888-515-3355*
≠ *(780) 439-1195*

The newly renovated Varscona offers guests king-size beds, wine and cheese upon arrival and a cozy fireplace for those cold Edmonton winters. In the heart of Old Strathcona, it is easily one of the city's best-located hotels.

Bagel Tree
$
10354 Whyte Ave
☎ *(780) 439-9604*

As one would expect, the Bagel Tree makes its own bagels. It also sells bagels imported from Fairmount Bagels in Montréal, arguably the best bagels around.

Barb and Ernie's
$
9906 72nd Ave.
☎ *(780) 433-3242*

This is an exceptionally popular diner-style restaurant with good food, good prices and a friendly, unpretentious ambience. Breakfast is a particularly busy time, so expect to have to wait a bit for a table

Old Strathcona 119

in the morning You can always come later, however, since breakfast is served until 4pm.

✗ Bee-Bell Health Bakery
$
10416 80th Ave.
☎ *(780) 439-3247*
Wonderful breads and pastries— what more can we say?

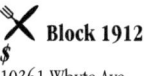

✗ Block 1912
$
10361 Whyte Ave.
☎ *(780) 433-6575*
Block 1912 is a European café that won an award for its effort to beautify the Strathcona area. The interior is like a living room with an eclectic mix of tables, chairs and sofas. Lasagna is one of the simple menu's best offerings. Soothing music and a relaxed mood are conducive to a chat with friends or the enjoyment of a good book.

✗ Funky Pickle Pizza Co.
$
10041 Whyte Ave.
☎ *(780) 433-3863*
At Funky Pickle Pizza Co., the art of pizza making is brought to unparalleled heights. Of course, at $3.50 a slice, it's not cheap. But the price is quickly forgotten as soon as your teeth sink into the whole-wheat crust, home-made sauce, blend of cheeses, fresh vegetables and spices – a sheer delight. Since the place is not much bigger than a counter, it's best to take out.

✗ Symposium
$$
10039 Whyte Ave.
☎ *(780) 433-7912*
Right above Funky Pickle Pizza is Symposium, a Greek restaurant whose pleasant terrace opens onto Whyte Avenue. The friendly staff serves dishes that go far beyond simply souvlaki and Greek salad. Try the shrimp salad on pita!

✗ Chianti Café
$$
10501 82nd Ave.
☎ *(780) 439-9829*
More than 20 varieties of pasta are served at Chianti Café located in Old Strathcona's former post office. Reservations are recommended on weekends.

Edmonton

Julio's Barrio
$$
10450 82nd Ave.
☎(780) 431-0774
Julio's boasts an original Mexican-Southwest decor with, cactus coat racks, soft leather chairs and *piñatas* hanging from the ceiling. The menu features a good selection of nachos and soups, plus all the regular Mexican fare. Servings are huge and the service is quick.

Packrat Louie Kitchen & Bar
$$
10335 83rd Ave.
☎(780) 433-0123
A good selection of wines and a nice atmosphere are mixed with interesting music. The menu offerings are varied and generally well prepared.

Turtle Creek
$$
8404 109th St.
☎(780) 433-4202
Turtle Creek is an Edmonton favourite for several reasons, not the least of which are its California wines and its relaxed ambiance. The dishes follow the latest trends in Californian and fusion cuisine very well, though a little predictably. The weekend brunch is a good deal. Free indoor parking.

The Unheardof Restaurant
$$$$
9602 82nd Ave.
☎(780) 432-0480
The name fits and it doesn't. This restaurant is no longer unheard of, yet it is an exception to Edmonton's dining norm. Recently expanded, it offers both à la carte and table d'hôte menus. While the menu changes every two weeks, it usually features fresh game in the fall and chicken or beef the rest of the year. Inventive vegetarian dishes are also available. The food is exquisite and refined. Reservations are required.

South of the North Saskatchewan River

Southbend Motel
$44
K, tv,
5130 Calgary Tr. Northbound, T6H 2H4
☎(780) 434-1418
⇌(780) 435-1525
For a very reasonable rate, guests can stay at the Southbend Motel where rooms are admittedly a bit dated. For no extra charge you can use all the facilities at the Best Western Cedar Park Inn next door (see below). These include a pool, a sauna and an exercise room.

South of the North Strathcona River 121

The Best Western Cedar Park Inn
$104-$149
≡, ℜ, ≈, △, ⊘, tv, ✈
5116 Calgary Tr. Northbound
☎ *(780) 434-7411*
☎ *800-661-9461*
☎ *800-528-1234*
₌ *(780) 437-4836*

The Cedar Park Inn is a large hotel with 190 equally spacious rooms. Some are called theme rooms *($150)*, which essentially means there is a hot-tub for two, a king-size bed, a living room and a fancier decor. Weekend and family rates are available. There is a courtesy limo service to the airports or the West Edmonton Mall.

Edmonton

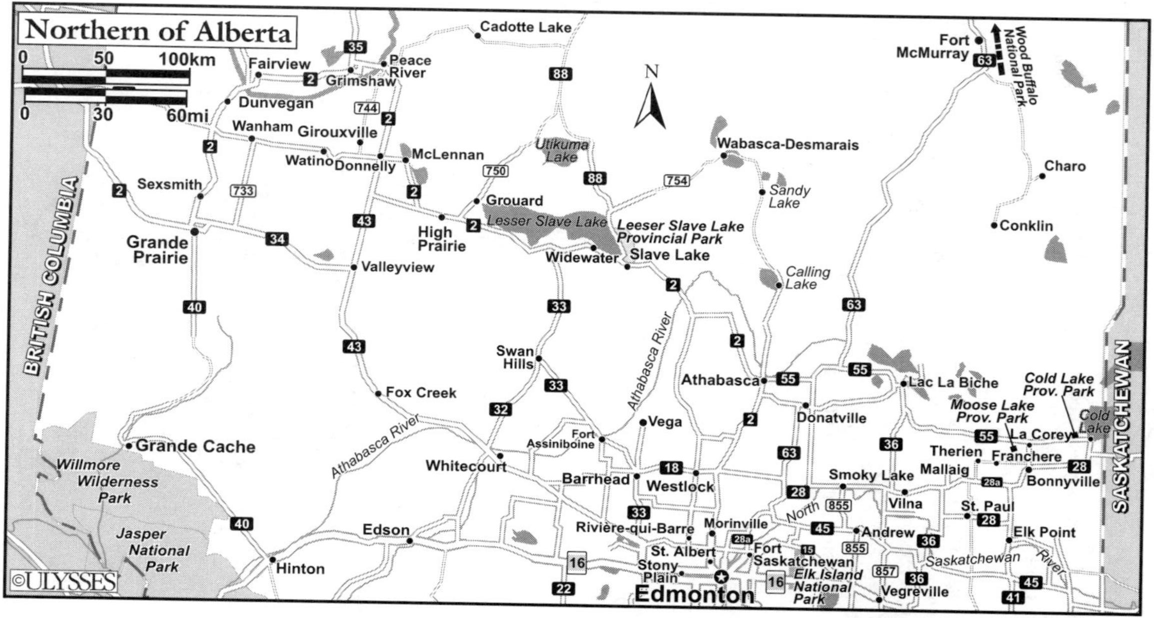
Northern of Alberta
0 50 100km
0 30 60mi
N
BRITISH COLUMBIA
SASKATCHEWAN
Cadotte Lake
Fairview
Peace River
Grimshaw
Dunvegan
Wanham
Girouxville
Watino
Donnelly
McLennan
Sexsmith
Grande Prairie
Valleyview
Utikuma Lake
Grouard
High Prairie
Lesser Slave Lake
Leeser Slave Lake Provincial Park
Widewater
Slave Lake
Wabasca-Desmarais
Sandy Lake
Calling Lake
Fort McMurray
Wood Buffalo National Park
Charo
Conklin
Swan Hills
Fox Creek
Athabasca River
Athabasca
Vega
Fort Assiniboine
Grande Cache
Willmore Wilderness Park
Jasper National Park
Whitecourt
Barrhead
Westlock
Donatville
Lac La Biche
Cold Lake Prov. Park
Moose Lake Prov. Park
Cold Lake
La Corey
Therien
Franchere
Mallaig
Bonnyville
Smoky Lake
Vilna
St. Paul
Elk Point
North Saskatchewan River
Andrew
Edson
Hinton
Rivière-qui-Barre
Morinville
St. Albert
Fort Saskatchewan
Stony Plain
Edmonton
Elk Island National Park
Vegreville
©ULYSSES

Northern Alberta

While Edmonton is the northernmost capital of the Canadian provinces, the vast stretch of land to its north still takes up more than half of Alberta's total area.

Before explorers and fur traders arrived, the region was occupied by Athapaskan and Cree Aboriginal peoples. Nomadic, they travelled on the Athabasca River, a route that would also link the huge territory of northern Alberta during the fur trade. On behalf of the North West Company, explorer David Thompson ventured up the Athabasca River in May 1799, soon to be followed by Peter Fidler with the rival Hudson Bay Company in January 1800. The province's first permanent European trading posts were later built here. As is the case throughout the province, the fur trade was replaced long ago by the oil and gas industry. The Athabasca oil sands make up the largest single deposit of oil in the world.

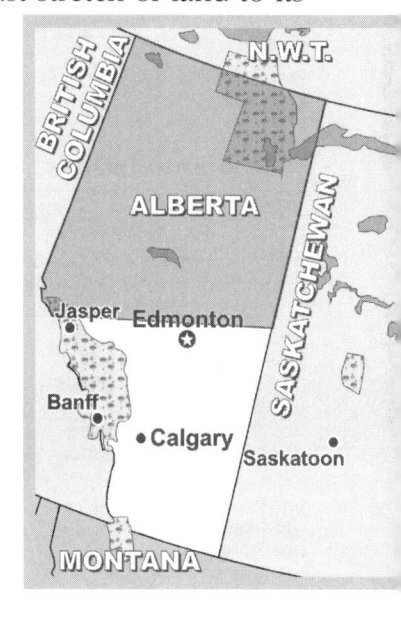

Though it remains an area with an extremely harsh winter climate and a sparse population, today it is a popular choice for both outdoor enthusiasts and Canadian history buffs. Massive lakes, rivers and forests cover the landscape, but the great distances between towns make touring the whole region difficult. That makes it all the more important to find a comfortable place to stay and a good meal at the end of an arduous day of travel.

Accommodations

Prices at the hotels, motels, inns and bed and breakfasts throughout northern Alberta are surprisingly reasonable for a northern region. Many of the inns and bed and breakfasts are situated in historic buildings. With the area's relatively thin population, it's extremely easy to find a quiet spot close to nature. Some of the historic inns are richly decorated in antique furnishings, giving guests a feel for the period. At the same time, there remain many modern, comfortable hotels and motels.

Suggestions for accommodations in this guide are listed for the towns of St. Paul, Smoky Lake, Cold Lake, Athabasca, Donatville, Lac La Biche, Fort McMurray, Slave Lake, Peace River and Grande Prairie.

Restaurants

While northern Alberta will never be considered a mecca for fine dining, there remain many simple and satisfying choices for hungry travellers. Eggs, bacon and pancakes for breakfast; a thick soup and sandwich for lunch; and a steak or burger for dinner could be a typical day of feasting. Not to worry though if you need a break from the hearty stuff: Greek, Italian, Spanish and Asian cuisine can be found in some of the larger towns.

The area's small-town restaurants are also popular meeting spots for locals and great places to soak up some of the regional atmosphere.

St. Paul

King's Motel and Restaurant
$48 bkfst incl.
≡, ℜ, ℝ, *tv*, &
5638 50th Ave., Box 1685, T0A 3A0
☎ *(780) 645-5656*
☎ *800-265-7407*
≠ *(780) 645-5107*
King's Motel offers decent, clean rooms, most of which have refrigerators. Breakfast at the restaurant is included

in the price. The motel's restaurant (*$*) serves hot pancakes and French toast breakfasts as well as lunch and dinner. The atmosphere is nothing special, but the food is good and inexpensive (breakfast is free if you're staying at the motel).

✕ Corfou Villa Restaurant
$$
5010 50th Ave.
☎*(780) 645-2948*
The Corfou serves Greek food, as its name suggests, but also dishes up Italian and Spanish specialities.

Smoky Lake

🛏 Countrylane Bed & Breakfast
$65
sb
Box 38, T0A 3C0, off Hwy 28, watch for signs at R.R. 36
☎*(780) 656-2277*
Each of the six rooms at the Countrylane Bed & Breakfast are named after the six girls that were born in the house. The sound of birds chirping and a sunny balcony are among the extras found throughout the rest of the house. An evening meal can be arranged with advance notice and group rates are available. An old schoolhouse dating from 1913 has now been renovated and added to Countrylane's facilities. It's an ideal spot to host business meetings or family celebrations.

🛏 Inn at the Ranch
$70
tv, ⊗
Box 562, T0A 3C0, Hwy. 855, 22km north of Hwy. 28, follow the signs
☎*(780) 656-2474*
☎*800-974-2474*
≠*(780) 656-3094*
Smoky Lake is home to another charming bed and breakfast, the Inn at the Ranch. This working bison-elk ranch has two lovely rooms. The newly built mansion is surrounded by a veritable bird-watcher's paradise.

Cold Lake

🍵 🛏 ✕ Harbour House B&B
$80
615 Lakeshore Dr.
☎*(780) 639-2337*
The Harbour House is a lovely spot on the shores of Cold Lake. Each room has a theme, ask for the one with the fireplace and canopy bed. A real gem! There is also an adjoining tea room. Each room now has its own bathroom. A family restaurant (*$*) offers breakfast, lunch and dinner. It serves light fare like sandwiches and cakes each afternoon.

Roundel Hotel
$-$$
902 Eighth Ave.
☎ *(780) 639-3261*
While not recommended as a place to stay, the Roundel Hotel serves standard fare all day long.

Athabasca

The Athabasca Inn
$99
≡, ℜ, ☺, tv, ✷
5211 41 Ave., T9S 1A5
☎ *(780) 675-2294*
☎ *800-567-5718*
⇌ *(780) 675-3890*
The Athabasca Inn features non-smoking rooms with filtered air. Business people make up the bulk of its guests. Rooms are clean and spacious.

Green Spot
$
4820 51st St.
☎ *(780) 675-3040*
The Green Spot is open from breakfast to dinner, serving a bit of everything from healthy soups and sandwiches (as its name suggests) to big juicy burgers.

Deer

Donatville

Donatberry Inn B&B
$75
⊛, △
R.R. 1, Boyle, T0A 0M0
☎ *(780) 689-3639*
⇌ *(780) 689-3380*
Located about halfway between Lac La Biche and Athabasca on Highway 63 is the small town of Donatville, home of the Donatberry Inn B&B. This newly built house is set on a large property with a northern berry orchard nearby (home-made preserves of these berries are served at breakfast). The large, bright rooms all have private bathrooms, and guests also have access to a whirlpool and a steam room.

Lac La Biche

Parkland Motel
$60
≡, K, tv, ⊛, ♿
9112 101 Ave., Box 659, T0A 2C0
☎ *(780) 623-4424*
☎ *888-884-8886*
⇌ *(780) 623-4599*
The Parkland Hotel features regular rooms and kitchenette suites, some of which have fireplaces and lofts. Good value.

Fort McMurray

Mackenzie Park Inn
$84
≡, ≈, ℜ, ⊛, tv, bar
424 Gregoire Dr., T9H 3R2
☎(780) 791-7200
☎800-582-3273
≠(780) 790-1658

With a good restaurant and lounge as well as a pool and a casino, the Mackenzie Park Inn is the most reliable hotel or motel choice in town. It is located about 4km (2.5mi) south of the centre of town. **Mapletree Pancake House $$** This restaurant is known for its huge Sunday brunch and, of course, its pancakes.

Garden Café
$
9924 Biggs Ave.
☎(780) 791-6665

This is a fresh and cheery place to enjoy soups, sandwiches and good desserts. It is open all day and all night.

Slave Lake

Sawridge Hotel
$75
≡, ℜ, △, ⊛, ℝ, tv, ☉, ♿
Box 879, T0G 2A0, just off Hwy 2 on Main St.
☎(780) 849-4101
☎800-661-6657
≠(780) 849-3426

The rather interesting exterior of the Sawridge Hotel houses some rather ordinary rooms that are just a tad outdated. Several of the rooms have refrigerators.

Northwest Inn
$84
ℝ, ≡, ℜ, K, ⊛, △, ☉, tv
Box 2459, T0G 2A0
☎(780) 849-3300
≠(780) 849-2667

Farther along Main Street towards town is the newest hotel in town, the Northwest Inn. The rooms, though clean and modern, are unfortunately very plain and bare. Some are equipped with refrigerators.

Joey's Incredible Edibles
$-$$
at the corner of Third Ave. and Main St.
☎(780) 849-5577

Joey's is a pleasant family-style restaurant with a complete menu including a wide choice of juicy hamburgers.

Peace River

Crescent Motor Inn Best Canadian
$49
≡, K, tv, ≈, ℜ
9810 98th St., T8S 1J3
☎(780) 624-2586
⇌(780) 624-1888

The Crescent Motor Inn is located close to the centre of town and offers clean, rather ordinary rooms. Family suites with kitchenettes are certainly an economical choice.

Kozy Quarters B&B
$60
sb
11015 99th St., Box 7493, T8S 1T1
☎(780) 624-2807

This historic two-storey structure is located on the waterfront. Built by the RCMP, today it houses cozy and spacious guest rooms. A choice of breakfasts is offered each morning.

Traveller's Motor Hotel
$61
≡, ℜ, K, △, tv, bar
Box 7290, T8S 1S9
☎(780) 624-3621
☎800-661-3227
⇌(780) 624-4855

The Traveller's Motor Hotel offers ordinary hotel-motel rooms as well as suite rooms. With a nightclub in the hotel, this isn't the quietest place in town. All rooms are newly renovated. Note that the price includes a special pass allowing free access to the golf course, municipal pool and the Peace River Sports Club.

Peace Garden
$$
10016 100th St.
☎(780) 624-1048

The best of the handful of Chinese restaurants in town, the Peace Garden serves good seafood dishes as well as North American standards like steak and pizza.

Grande Prairie

Canadian Motor Inn
$62
≡, ℜ, K, tv, ⊛, 🐾
10901 100th Ave., T8V 3J9
☎(780) 532-1680
☎800-291-7893
⇌(780) 532-1245

Grande Prairie's best hotel and motel bet is the Canadian Motor Inn where each room has two queen-size beds, a refrigerator and a large-screen television. Rooms with fully equipped kitchenettes are available (*$68*). There is also an executive suite with a whirlpool bath (*$150-$200*). The hotel was recently completely renovated resulting in a spotless, modern, yet very comfortable accommodations.

Grande Prairie

🛏 Fieldstone Inn B&B
$80 bkfst incl.
Box 295, T8V 3A4
☎ *(780) 532-7529*

Set on a secluded lakeside property, the Fieldstone Inn B&B is a great find, as long as you have no problem with their new "celebrating marriage" policy whereby unmarried couples must stay in separate rooms. This newly built fieldstone house has a homey feel, thanks to the old-fashioned decor and classic styling. Some rooms have whirlpool baths or fireplaces. The balcony is an ideal spot to contemplate the rose garden and, if you're lucky, the northern lights.

🛏 Golden Inn
$84
≡, ℜ, K, tv, bar
11201 100th Ave., T8V 5M6
☎ *(780) 539-6000*
☎ *800-661-7954*
≠ *(780) 532-1961*

The Golden Inn lies north of the city centre with services and shops nearby. The decor of the rooms and lobby is slightly outdated.

🍴 Java Junction
$
9931 100th Ave.
☎ *(780) 539-5070*

Java Junction is a funky spot in the small downtown area with hearty and inexpensive muffins, soups and sandwiches.

🍴 Earl's
$$
9825 100th St.
☎ *(780) 538-3275*

Grande Prairie is home to one of Alberta's several Earl's restaurant outlets. With its outdoor terrace and reliable and varied menu, it is a favourite in town.

Northern Alberta

Accommodation Index

Alberta Suite Hotel (Edmonton) 111
Alpine Club of Canada (Canmore) 18
Alpine Village (Jasper) . 43
Ambleside Lodge (Canmore) 18
Amethyst Lodge (Jasper) 39
Art Deco Heritage House B&B (Lethbridge) ... 89
Astoria Hotel (Jasper) .. 38
Athabasca Hotel (Jasper) 38
Badlands Motel (Drumheller) 100
Banff Rocky Mountain Resort (Banff) 26
Banff Springs Hotel (Banff) 27
Banff Voyager Inn (Banff) 24
Bartlett House B&B (Lethbridge) 91
Becker's Chalets (Jasper) 42
Best Western Heidelberg Inn (Lethbridge) 91
Best Western Airport (Calgary) 77
Best Western Cedar Park Inn (Edmonton) 121
Best Western City Centre (Edmonton) 111
Best Western Green Gables Inn (Canmore) 19
Best Western Inn (Medicine Hat) 95
Best Western Jurassic Inn (Drumheller) 101
Best Western Kananaskis Inn (Kananaskis) ... 50
Best Western Port O' Call Inn (Calgary) 78
Best Western Suites Calgary Centre (Calgary) 57
Best Western Village Park Inn (Calgary) 80
Best Western Westwood Inn (Edmonton) ... 116
Black Cat Guest Ranch (Hinton) 44
Bow View Motor Lodge (Banff) 24
Brewster's Mountain Lodge (Banff) 27
Calgary Mariott Hotel (Calgary) 58
Canadian Motor Inn (Grande Prairie) ... 128
Caribou Lodge (Banff) . 25
Carriage House Inn (Calgary) 69
Castle Mountain Village (Banff) 32
Chateau Jasper (Jasper) . 40
Chateau Lake Louise (Lake Louise) 33
Columbia Icefield Chalet (Icefields Parkway) . 36
Columbia Valley Lodge (Golden) 50
Comfort Inn (Calgary) .. 79
Commercial Hotel (Edmonton) 118
Cougar Canyon B&B (Canmore) 18
Countrylane Bed & Breakfast (Smoky Lake) .. 125
Crandell Mountain Lodge (Waterton) 85
Crescent Motel (Radium Hot Springs) 46
Crescent Motor Inn Best Canadian (Peace River) ... 128
Crystal Springs Motel (Radium Hot Springs) 46

Accommodation Index

David Thompson Resort (Nordegg) 104
Days Inn (Calgary) 79
Days Inn (Lethbridge) .. 91
Days Inn Downtown (Edmonton) 110
Deer Lodge (Lake Louise) 33
Delphine Lodge (Invermere) 49
Delta Bow Valley (Calgary) 60
Delta Edmonton Centre Suite Hotel (Edmonton) 114
Dickens Inn (Cochrane) 103
Donatberry Inn B&B (Donatville) 126
Douglas Country Inn (Brooks) 100
Douglas Fir Resort & Chalets (Banff) 26
Econo Lodge (Calgary) . 79
Econo Lodge (Edmonton) 110
Edmonton West Travelodge (Edmonton) 117
Edmonton Westin Hotel (Edmonton) 111
Elbow River Inn (Calgary) 68
Emerald Lake Lodge (Yoho National Park) 49
Fairmont Hot Springs Resort (Fairmont Hot Springs) 48
Fantasyland Hotel & Resort (Edmonton) . 117
Fieldstone Inn B&B (Grande Prairie) ... 129
Georgetown Inn (Canmore) 19
Ginger Tea Room and Gift Shop (Okotoks) . 88
Golden Inn (Grande Prairie) ... 129

Grand Hotel (Edmonton) 110
Greenwood Inn (Calgary) 78
Groves B&B (Medicine Hat) 93
Harbour House B&B (Cold Lake) 125
Heartwood Manor (Drumheller) 101
High Country Inn (Banff) 26
Highlander Hotel (Calgary) 79
Holgate House B&B (Edmonton) 117
Holiday Inn Calgary Downtown (Calgary) 57
Holiday Inn Express (Calgary) 80
Holiday Lodge (Banff) . 22
Homestead Inn (Banff) . 22
Hotel MacDonald (Edmonton) 114
Inglewood Bed & Breakfast (Calgary) .. 65
Inn at the Ranch (Smoky Lake) 125
Inn on Seventh (Edmonton) 111
Inns of Banff, Rundle Manor (Banff) 24
Inns of Banff, Swiss Village (Banff) 24
Jasper House (Jasper) .. 43
Jasper Inn (Jasper) 39
Jasper Park Lodge (Jasper) 40
Johnston Canyon Resort (Banff) 30
King Edward Hotel (Banff) 22
King's Motel and Restaurant (St. Paul) 124
Kootenay Park Lodge (Kootenay National Park) 46

Accommodation Index

Kosy Knest Kabins (Crowsnest Pass) ... 85
Kozy Quarters B&B (Peace River) 128
La Boheme B&B (Edmonton) 118
Lady MacDonald Country Inn (Canmore) 19
Lake Louise Inn (Lake Louise) 32
Lethbridge Lodge Hotel (Lethbridge) 91
Levis by the River (Edmonton) 115
Lobstick Lodge (Jasper) 39
Lodge at Kananaskis & The Kananaskis Hotel (Kananaskis) 51
London Road B&B (Lethbridge) 89
Mackenzie Park Inn (Fort McMurray) ... 127
Maligne Lodge (Jasper) . 38
Marmot Lodge (Jasper) . 39
McIntosh Tea House Bed and Breakfast (Red Deer) 104
McLaren Lodge (Golden) 50
Medicine Hat Lodge (Medicine Hat) 95
Memories Inn (Longview) 89
Miette Hot Spring Bungalows (Miette Hot Springs) 44
Misty River Lodge (Radium Hot Springs) 46
Moraine Lake Lodge (Lake Louise) 33
Motel Tyrol (Radium Hot Springs) 48
Mount Royal Hotel (Banff) 28
Mountaineer Lodge (Lake Louise) 32
Newcastle Country Inn (Drumheller) 100
Norquay's Timberline Inn (Banff) 21
Northwest Inn (Slave Lake) 127
Num-Ti-Jah Lodge (Icefields Parkway) . 34
Overlander Mountain Lodge (Hinton) 45
Panorama Resort (Invermere) 49
Paradise Lodge & Bungalows (Lake Louise) 32
Park Avenue Bed & Breakfast (Banff) ... 24
Parkland Motel (Lac La Biche) 126
Patricia Lake Bungalows (Jasper) 36
Pine Bungalow Cabins (Jasper) 43
Pocahontas Bungalows (Miette Hot Springs) . 44
Pointe Inn (Calgary) ... 77
Post Hotel (Lake Louise) 33
Prestige Inn (Golden) .. 50
Prince of Wales Hotel (Waterton) 87
Prince Royal Inn (Calgary) 57
Private Accommodation at the Knauers' (Jasper) 36
Ptarmigan Inn (Banff) .. 26
Pyramid Lake Resort (Jasper) 43
Quality Hotel and Conference Centre (Calgary) 56
Quality Inn Motel Village (Calgary) 80
Radium Hot Springs Lodge (Radium Hot Springs) ... 48
Ramada Crownchild Inn (Calgary) 57
Red Carpet Inn (Banff) . 21

Accommodation Index

Red Carpet Motor Hotel (Calgary) 79
Red Deer Lodge (Red Deer) 105
Rimrock Resort Hotel (Banff) 27
Ripley Ridge Manor (Calgary) 65
Rocky Mountain Ski Lodge (Canmore) 19
Rosebud Country (Rosebud) 102
Rundle Manor (Banff) .. 24
Rundle Mountain Motel & Gasthaus (Canmore) 18
Rundle Stone Lodge (Banff) 25
Sandman Hotel (Calgary) 57
Sandman Inn (Lethbridge) 91
Sawridge Hotel (Jasper) .. 41
Sawridge Hotel (Slave Lake) 127
Sheraton Suites Calgary Eau Claire (Calgary) . 58
Skoki Lodge (Lake Louise) 32
Skyline Accommodation (Jasper) 36
Southbend Motel (Edmonton) 120
St. Ann Ranch (Trochu) 102
Storm Mountain Lodge (Kootenay National Park) 46
Strathcona Hotel (Edmonton) 118
Suite Dreams B&B (Hinton) 44
Swiss Village (Banff) ... 24
Sylvan Lake Bed & Breakfast (Sylvan Lake) ... 103
Tannanhof Pension (Banff) 25

Taste the Past B&B (Drumheller) 100
Tekkara Lodge (Jasper) . 40
Tel-Star Motor Inn (Brooks) 98
The Athabasca Inn (Athabaska) 126
The Blackfoot Inn (Calgary) 69
The Chalet (Radium Hot Springs) 48
The Creek House (Canmore) 20
The Crossing (Icefields Parkway) . 34
The Edmonton House Suite Hotel (Edmonton) 112
The Inn on Fourth (Medicine Hat) 95
The Inn on the Lake (Crowsnest Pass) ... 84
The Kilmorey Lodge (Waterton) 85
The Lodge at Waterton (Waterton) 87
The Lord Nelson Inn (Calgary) 56
The Mackenzie House Bed and Breakfast (Fort Macleod) ... 88
The Northland Lodge (Waterton) 85
The Palliser (Calgary) .. 60
The Red Coat Inn (Fort Macleod) 88
The Rose Country Inn (Wetaskiwin) 106
The Sunny Holme B&B (Medicine Hat) 93
Tonquin Inn (Jasper) .. 38
Traveller's Inn (Banff) .. 25
Traveller's Motor Hotel (Peace River) 128
Tunnel Mountain Chalets (Banff) 27

134 Accommodation Index

Union Bank Inn Hotel
  (Edmonton) 112
Varscona (Edmonton) . 118
Voyageur Motel
  (Rocky Mountain
    House) 104
Waldorf Hotel
  (Drumheller) 100

Walking Eagle Motor Inn
  (Rocky Mountain
    House) 104
West Harvest Inn
  (Edmonton) 116
Whistler Inn (Jasper) ... 38

Restaurant Index

4th Street Rose (Calgary) 73
Albert's Family Restaurant
   (Edmonton) 115
Alpine Village (Jasper) . 43
Amethyst Lodge (Jasper) 39
Anton's (Lethbridge) ... 92
At Damon Lane's
   Tearoom
      (Medicine Hat) ... 95
Athena Pizza (Banff) ... 29
Athens Corner Restaurant
   (Hinton) 45
Bagel Tree (Edmonton) 118
Balkan Restaurant
   (Banff) 29
Baraka Café
   (Edmonton) 114
Barb and Ernie's
   (Edmonton) 118
Barley Mill (Calgary) .. 66
Bear's Paw Bakery
   (Jasper) 41
Beauvallon Dining Room
   (Jasper) 40
Beauvert Dining Room
   (Jasper) 41
Becker's Chalets (Jasper) 42
Bee-Bell Health Bakery
   (Edmonton) 119
Beeline Chicken & Pizza
   (Lake Louise) 34
Best Western Kananaskis
   Inn (Kananaskis) ... 50
Big Rock Grill (Calgary) 71
Bistro Praha
   (Edmonton) 115
Block 1912 (Edmonton) 119
Blue House Cafe
   (Calgary) 80
Borderline (Waterton) .. 87
Boston Pizza (Canmore) 20
Break the Fast Cafe
   (Calgary) 60

Brewster Brewing
   Company and
   Restaurant (Calgary) . 71
Buchanan's (Calgary) .. 68
Buon Giorno (Calgary) . 71
Buzzard's Cowboy Cuisine
   (Calgary) 72
Byblos Kitchen (Calgary) 69
Caboose (Banff) 30
Caesar's Steakhouse
   (Calgary) 64
Café Orleans
   (Edmonton) 115
Café Select
   (Edmonton) 115
Cajun Charlie's
   (Calgary) 66
Cannery Row (Calgary) . 76
Cantonese Restaurant
   (Jasper) 42
Caribou Lodge (Banff) . 25
Caroline's Pub & Eatery
   (Medicine Hat) 96
Carver's Steakhouse
   (Calgary) 78
Cedar's Deli (Calgary) .. 60
Celadon Cafe and Lounge
   (Calgary) 71
Chateau Jasper (Jasper) . 40
Chateau Lake Louise
   (Lake Louise) 33
Cheesecake Café
   (Red Deer) 106
Cheesecake Café Bakery
   Restaurant
      (Edmonton) 114
Chez François
   (Canmore) 21
Chianti (Calgary) 69
Chianti Café
   (Edmonton) 119
Chief Chiniki
   (Kananaskis) 51
Cilantro (Calgary) 75

Restaurant Index

City Roast Coffee (Red Deer) 105
Claude's on the River (Edmonton) 116
Coco Pazzo (Lethbridge) 92
Coco's Café (Jasper) ... 41
Corfou Villa Restaurant (St. Paul) 125
Cupper's (Lethbridge) .. 92
Da Paolo Ristorante (Calgary) 72
Deane House Restaurant (Calgary) 66
Deer Lodge (Lake Louise) 33
Delectable Delights (Calgary) 70
Denjiro (Jasper) 42
Divino (Calgary) 61
Drinkwaters Grill (Calgary) 61
Earl's (Grande Prairie) 129
Earl's Tin Palace (Calgary) 72
Econo Lodge (Calgary) . 79
Edelweiss Dining Room (Lake Louise) 33
Ed's Restaurant (Calgary) 71
Embarcadero Wine and Oyster Bar (Calgary) . 72
Emerald Lake Lodge (Yoho National Park) 49
Entre Nous (Calgary) .. 75
Escoba Cafe and Bar (Calgary) 62
Fairmont Hot Springs Resort (Fairmont Hot Springs) 48
Fiore Cantina Italiana (Calgary) 73
Fireside Dining Room (Hinton) 45
Florentine (Calgary) ... 73
Forbidden Flavours (Calgary) 70
Funky Pickle Pizza Co. (Edmonton) 119

Galaxie Diner (Calgary) 70
Garden Café (Fort McMurray) ... 127
Garden Court Dining Room (Waterton) ... 87
Good Earth Cafe (Calgary) 65
Good Food Company (Red Deer) 105
Grand Isle (Calgary) ... 66
Greek Classic (Lloydminster) 106
Green Spot (Athabaska) 126
Greentree Café (Hinton) 45
Grizzly House (Banff) .. 29
Harbour House B&B (Cold Lake) 125
Home Quarter Restaurant & Pie Shoppe (Cochrane) 103
Husky House (Calgary) . 70
Hy's (Calgary) 64
Hy's Steakloft (Edmonton) 116
Indochine (Calgary) ... 64
Inn on Lake Bonavista (Calgary) 77
Jasper Inn (Jasper) 39
Jasper Park (Jasper) ... 40
Jasper Pizza Place (Jasper) 42
Java Junction (Grande Prairie) ... 129
Joe BTFSPLK's (Banff) . 28
Joey Tomato's (Calgary) 67
Joey's Incredible Edibles (Slave Lake) 127
Joey's Only (Calgary) .. 73
Julio's Barrio (Edmonton) 120
Khublai (Calgary) 73
King's Motel and Restaurant (St. Paul) 124
Kootenay Park Lodge (Kootenay National Park) 46

Restaurant Index

Korean Restaurant
(Banff) 29
Kremlin (Calgary) 74
L&W Restaurant (Jasper) 42
La Bohème
(Edmonton) 118
La Brezza Ristorante
(Calgary) 67
La Caille on the Bow
(Calgary) 68
La Chaumiere (Calgary) 77
La P'tite Table (Okotoks) 89
Lake Louise Grill & Bar
(Lake Louise) 34
Le Beaujolais (Banff) . . 30
Lethbridge Lodge Hotel
(Lethbridge) 91
Levis by the River
(Edmonton) 115
Lodge at Kananaskis &
The Kananaskis Hotel
(Kananaskis) 51
Lunch at Lorna's
(Lloydminster) . . . 106
L'Escapade (Kananaskis) 51
Mackay's Ice Cream
(Cochrane) 103
Mackenzie Park Inn
(Fort McMurray) . . . 127
Madison Grill
(Edmonton) 112
Magpie & Stump (Banff) 29
Mamma's Restaurant
(Medicine Hat) 95
Mamma's Ristorante
(Calgary) 81
Manifesto (Edmonton) 114
Mapletree Pancake House
(Fort McMurray) . . . 127
McQueen's Upstairs
(Calgary) 76
Medicine Hat Lodge
(Medicine Hat) 95
Mescalero (Calgary) . . . 76
Miss Italia Ristorante
(Jasper) 41

Modern Art Café
(Edmonton) 115
Mongolie Grill (Calgary) 74
Moraine Lake Lodge
(Lake Louise) 33
Moti Mahal (Calgary) . . 74
Mount Engadine Lodge
(Kananaskis) 51
Naturbahn Teahouse
(Calgary) 80
Nellie's Kitchen
(Calgary) 70
Num-Ti-Jah Lodge
(Icefields Parkway) . 34
Nutter's (Canmore) 20
Obsessions
(Kananaskis) 51
Outwest (Calgary) 67
Overlander Mountain
Lodge (Hinton) 45
Owl's Nest (Calgary) . . . 65
O'Sho Japanese
Restaurant
(Lethbridge) 92
Pacific Fish
(Edmonton) 115
Packrat Louie Kitchen &
Bar (Edmonton) . . . 120
Panorama Dining Room
(Calgary) 64
Peace Garden
(Peace River) 128
Pegasus (Calgary) 71
Peggy Sue's Diner
(Brooks) 100
Peppermill (Canmore) . 21
Peter's Drive-In
(Calgary) 78
Piq Niq Cafe (Calgary) . 60
Pizza Hut (Hinton) 45
Plantier's (Edmonton) . 115
Post Hotel (Lake Louise) 33
Prestige Inn (Golden) . . 50
Primal Grounds
(Calgary) 70
Prince of Wales Hotel
(Waterton) 87

Restaurant Index

Pyramid Lake Resort
(Jasper) 43
Radium Hot Springs
(Radium Hot Springs) 48
Rajdoot (Calgary) 74
Ranchers (Hinton) 45
Rimrock Room (Calgary) 65
River Cafe (Calgary) . . . 67
Rose & Crown Pub
(Calgary) 71
Rose and Crown (Banff) 28
Roundel Hotel
(Cold Lake) 126
Rustler's (Medicine Hat) 96
Sam's Original Restaurant
and Bar (Calgary) . . . 66
Santa Lucia (Canmore) . 20
Savoir Fare (Calgary) . . 75
Schwartzie's Bagel
Noshery (Calgary) . . 61
Shanghaï (Lethbridge) . . 93
Sherlock Holmes
(Edmonton) 115
Showdowns Eatin'
Adventures
(Lethbridge) 93
Silver Dragon (Calgary) . 67
Silver Dragon Restaurant
(Banff) 29
Sinclairs (Canmore) . . . 21
Sizzling House
(Drumheller) 102
Smitty's Restaurant
(Jasper) 41
Smuggler's Inn (Calgary) 75
Soft Rock Internet Cafe
(Jasper) 41
Spooner's Coffee Bar
(Jasper) 42
Storm Mountain Lodge
(Kootenay National
Park) 46
Stromboli Inn (Calgary) . 67
Sukiyaki House (Banff) . 30
Sukiyaki House
(Calgary) 75
Sultan's Tent (Calgary) . 76

Sunterra Bistro (Calgary) 61
Sunterra Market
(Calgary) 61
Sunterra Marketplace
(Calgary) 61
Sven Ericksen's
(Lethbridge) 93
Symposium
(Edmonton) 119
Syrtaki Greek Restaurant
(Edmonton) 117
Taj Mahal (Calgary) . . . 72
Teatro (Calgary) 64
Thai Sa-On (Calgary) . . 75
The Bridge
(Drumheller) 101
The Cake Company
(Banff) 28
The City Bakery
(Medicine Hat) 95
The Corner Stop
Restaurant
(Drumheller) . . . 101
The Crossing
(Icefields Parkway) . 34
The Embassy (Calgary) . 62
The Garden Café
(Lethbridge) 92
The Jasper Marketplace
(Jasper) 42
The Kabin (Canmore) . . 20
The Keg (Banff) 25
The Kilmorey Lodge
(Waterton) 85
The King & I Thai
Restaurant (Calgary) . 73
The Lamp Post Dining
Room (Waterton) . . . 85
The MacEachern Tea
House & Restaurant
(Wetaskiwin) . . . 106
The Penny Coffee House
(Lethbride) 92
The Rosebud Dinner
Theatre (Rosebud) . 102
The Silver Grill
(Fort Macleod) 88

The Unheardof Restaurant
(Edmonton) 120
The Waterton Park Café
(Waterton) 88
Ticino (Banff) 30
Turtle Creek
(Edmonton) 120
Valerie's Tea Room
(Waterton) 87

Victoria's Restaurant
(Calgary) 74
Virginia's (Calgary) 76
Virginia's Market Cafe
(Calgary) 72
Windsor Lounge
(Waterton) 87
Yavis Family Restaurant
(Drumheller) 101

Place Index

Athabasca	126
Banff	21
Brooks	98
Calgary	53
Along the Bow River	65
Downtown	56
North	77
South	68
Canmore	18
Cochrane	103
Cold Lake	125
Crowsnest Pass	84
Donatville	126
Drumheller	100
Edmonton	107
Downtown	110
East of Downtown	117
Old Strathcona	118
South of the North Saskatchewan River	120
West of Downtown	116
Fairmont Hot Springs	48
Fort Macleod	88
Fort McMurray	127
Golden	50
Grande Prairie	128
Hinton	44
Icefields Parkway	34
Invermere	49
Jasper	36
Kananaskis Country	50
Kootenay National Park	46
Lac La Biche	126
Lake Louise	32
Lethbridge	89
Lloydminster	106
Longview	89
Medicine Hat	93
Miette Hot Springs	44
Nordegg	104
Northern Alberta	123
Okotoks	88
Peace River	128
Radium Hot Springs	46
Red Deer	104
Rocky Mountain House	104
Rosebud	102
Slave Lake	127
Smoky Lake	125
Southern Alberta	83
St. Paul	124
Sylvan Lake	103
Trochu	102
Waterton	85
Wetaskiwin	106
Yoho National Park	49

ULYSSES Travel Guides

Travel better, enjoy more

Surf our site to travel better, enjoy more

www.ulyssesguides.com

For enlightened travel

Order Form

Ulysses Travel Guides

- ☐ Acapulco . . . . . $14.95 CAN / $9.95 US
- ☐ Atlantic Canada $24.95 CAN / $17.95 US
- ☐ Bahamas . . . . . $24.95 CAN / $17.95 US
- ☐ Beaches of Maine $12.95 CAN / $9.95 US
- ☐ Bed & Breakfasts in Québec $14.95 CAN / $10.95 US
- ☐ Belize . . . . $16.95 CAN / $12.95 US
- ☐ Calgary . . . . . . $17.95 CAN / $12.95 US
- ☐ Canada . . . . $29.95 CAN / $21.95 US
- ☐ Chicago . . . . . . $19.95 CAN / $14.95 US
- ☐ Chile . . . . $27.95 CAN / $17.95 US
- ☐ Colombia . . . . . $29.95 CAN / $21.95 US
- ☐ Costa Rica . . . . $27.95 CAN / $19.95 US
- ☐ Cuba . . . . $24.95 CAN / $17.95 US
- ☐ Dominican Republic $24.95 CAN / $17.95 US
- ☐ Ecuador and Galápagos Islands $24.95 CAN / $17.95 US
- ☐ El Salvador . . . . $22.95 CAN / $14.95 US
- ☐ Guadeloupe . . . $24.95 CAN / $17.95 US
- ☐ Guatemala . . . . $24.95 CAN / $17.95 US
- ☐ Hawaii . . . . $29.95 CAN / $21.95 US
- ☐ Honduras . . . . . $24.95 CAN / $17.95 US
- ☐ Islands of the Bahamas $24.95 CAN / $17.95 US
- ☐ Las Vegas . . . . . $17.95 CAN / $12.95 US
- ☐ Lisbon . . . . $18.95 CAN / $13.95 US
- ☐ Louisiana . . . . . $29.95 CAN / $21.95 US
- ☐ Martinique . . . . $24.95 CAN / $17.95 US
- ☐ Montréal . . . . . $19.95 CAN / $14.95 US
- ☐ Miami . . . . $9.95 CAN / $12.95 US
- ☐ New Orleans . . $17.95 CAN / $12.95 US
- ☐ New York City . $19.95 CAN / $14.95 US
- ☐ Nicaragua . . . . . $24.95 CAN / $16.95 US
- ☐ Ontario . . . . . . $27.95 CAN / $19.95 US
- ☐ Ontario's Best Hotels and Restaurants . . . $27.95 CAN / $19.95 US
- ☐ Ottawa . . . . $17.95 CAN / $12.95 US
- ☐ Panamá . . . . . . $24.95 CAN / $17.95 US
- ☐ Peru . . . . $27.95 CAN / $19.95 US
- ☐ Phoenix . . . . . . $16.95 CAN / $12.95 US
- ☐ Portugal . . . . . . $24.95 CAN / $16.95 US
- ☐ Provence - Côte d'Azur $29.95 CAN / $21.95 US
- ☐ Puerto Rico . . . $24.95 CAN / $17.95 US
- ☐ Québec . . . . . . $29.95 CAN / $21.95 US
- ☐ Québec City . . . $17.95 CAN / $12.95 US
- ☐ Québec and Ontario with Via . . . . $9.95 CAN / $7.95 US

- ☐ Seattle ...... $17.95 CAN / $12.95 US
- ☐ Toronto ...... $18.95 CAN / $13.95 US
- ☐ Tunisia .... $27.95 CAN / $19.95 US
- ☐ Vancouver .... $17.95 CAN / $12.95 US
- ☐ Washington D.C. $18.95 CAN / $13.95 US
- ☐ Western Canada $29.95 CAN / $21.95 US

Ulysses Due South

- ☐ Acapulco ..... $14.95 CAN / $9.95 US
- ☐ Belize .... $16.95 CAN / $12.95 US
- ☐ Cancún & Riviera Maya ..... $19.95 CAN / $14.95 US
- ☐ Cartagena (Colombia) ..... $12.95 CAN / $9.95 US
- ☐ Huatulco - Puerto Escondido $17.95 CAN / $12.95 US
- ☐ Los Cabos and La Paz .... $14.95 CAN / $10.95 US
- ☐ Puerto Plata - Sosua ..... $14.95 CAN / $9.95 US
- ☐ Puerto Vallarta . $14.95 CAN / $9.95 US
- ☐ St. Martin and St. Barts ..... $16.95 CAN / $12.95 US

Ulysses Travel Journals

- ☐ Ulysses Travel Journal (Blue, Red, Green, Yellow, Sextant) .... $9.95 CAN / $7.95 US
- ☐ Ulysses Travel Journal (80 Days) ..... $14.95 CAN / $9.95 US

Ulysses Green Escapes

- ☐ Cycling in France $22.95 CAN / $16.95 US
- ☐ Cycling in Ontario $22.95 CAN / $16.95 US
- ☐ Hiking in the Northeastern U.S. $19.95 CAN / $13.95 US
- ☐ Hiking in Québec $19.95 CAN / $13.95 US

Title	Qty	Price	Total

Name:

Subtotal

Shipping $4 CAN

Address:

Subtotal

GST in Canada 7%

Total

Tel: Fax:

E-mail:

Payment: ☐ Cheque ☐ Visa ☐ MasterCard

Card number_____

Expiry date_____

Signature_____

ULYSSES TRAVEL GUIDES

4176 St-Denis,
Montréal, Québec,
H2W 2M5
(514) 843-9447
fax (514) 843-9448

305 Madison Avenue,
Suite 1166,
New York, NY 10165

Toll free: 1-877-542-7247
Info@ulysses.ca
www.ulyssesguides.com